Gender

Qualities, Quirks, and Quarrels

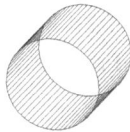

Author's Books

(As at 2016)

Non fiction

The Nature of Love and Relationships 2011, **2016** 2nd Edition
Doubts and Decisions for Living:
   Volume I: The Foundation of Human Thoughts **2014**
   Volume II: The Sanctity of Human Spirit **2014**
   Volume III: The Structure of Human Life **2014**
Relationship Facts, Trends, and Choices **2016**
The Mysteries of Life, Love, and Happiness **2016**
Marriage and Divorce Hardships **2016**
Gender Qualities, Quirks, and Quarrels **2016**
Relationship Needs, Framework, and Models **2016**

Fiction

Persian Moons **2007, 2016** 2nd Edition
Midnight Gate-opener 2011, **2016** 2nd Edition
My Lousy Life Stories **2014**

Love and Relationships Series
The war of Sexes

Gender
Qualities,
Quirks,
and *Quarrels*

Tom Omidi, Ph.D.

Love and Relationships Series # 4
Copyright © 2016 by Tom Omidi

Library and Archives Canada Cataloguing in Publication

Omidi, Tom, 1945-
Gender qualities, quirks, and quarrels : the war of sexes
/ Tom Omidi.

(Love and relationships series ; 4)
ISBN 978-0-9938006-8-9 (paperback)

1. Sex (Psychology). 2. Sex differences (Psychology).
3. Interpersonal relations. 4. Man-woman relationships. I. Title.

BF692.2.O45 2016   155.3'3   C2016-902407-5

Published by Eros Books,
Vancouver, British Columbia
Canada
contact@erosbooks.net

Printed in the United States

Contents

Contents (Cont.)

INTRODUCTION

HUMAN species is incredible in so many ways, including aptitude, attitude, logic, mentality, sentimentality, creativity, cruelty, etc. The multidimensionality of our character is just amazing, especially in the ways we combine these attributes so artfully often with no obvious consistency. All these special talents make our heads spin and wonder whether any aliens, even if they existed, could compete with humans in terms of the vast variety of attributes that we behold.

A multi-volume book about our qualities, quirks, and quarrels would be quite educational, entertaining, and sad in many respects. A few of those volumes only about 'human interactions' would be especially interesting already. However, the matter becomes ten folds more perplexing when we explore gender encounters and differences. In particular, the often-disturbing effects of these differences in marital relationships make us question God's wisdom to create men and women so differently. Therefore, this topic is briefly tackled in this book. Naturally, people perceive events and people according to their unique personalities. However, it also appears that men and women have major, yet uniform, differences in terms of mentality, perceptions, priorities, and interpreting life.

We have personally felt the gender divergence in mentality and attitude, and history supports our observations too. While genders' physical and hormonal differences are obvious, their behavioural and emotional differences have been a matter of curiosity, excitement, and irritation regularly, especially in the new era. Even more amazing, the more we have tried to learn about, and practice, gender equality, the more gender differences have manifested and the more conflicts have risen between men and women.

Overall, as relationship conundrums increase in society, we feel both obliged and intrigued to study gender mentalities and answer questions like the followings:

1. Are gender differences significant enough to measure and validate?
2. What kinds of effects these differences have on people's lives and happiness?
3. How much of the differences are useful or harmful for both personal welfare and interacting with the opposite sex?
4. What is the importance of knowing these differences?
5. How much of the differences are genetics?
6. How much of the differences are due to cultural and lifestyle influences?
7. How much of the differences are the results of variations in genders' perceptions of the world and life?
8. Are increasing misperceptions about the purpose of life and lifestyles alienating genders?
9. Is the increasing shallowness of social values going to drive gender differences and conflicts to the extreme?
10. Are these differences consistent across all humans around the globe or change due to culture and lifestyles?

This book would emphasize mainly on the first four questions to the extent our review might help relationships. In particular, the discussions in the following chapters about these questions lead to five main conclusions:

A. Men and women think, feel, and behave differently in general, although they follow the same logical and behavioural patterns on many occasions as well.

B. While these differences are noticeable and studied for the overall population, they do no necessarily apply to all men or women. Plenty of exceptions exist regarding the general observations made in this book.

C. Gender differences make a substantial impact on couples' relationships both positively and negatively.

D. These differences weaken the fundamentals of social structure, hinder teamwork in families, and reduce the chance of personal happiness.

E. The main importance of knowing about these differences is to raise couples' sensitivity about the symptoms of gender differences, which they must face realistically as inherent features of their relationships. In fact, this knowledge could help them take better advantage of those gender differences once they set their mindsets properly.

PART I

Gender Qualities

CHAPTER ONE
Human Personality

IN order to understand gender differences, we must know a little bit about human personality in general. Then, we can study gender differences according to various dimensions of human personality. As a first step, we can signify and measure someone's personality in terms of how effectively he/she can:

a) apply his/her **instincts**,
b) reason and use his/her **logic**,
c) connect with people and society—**Model**, and
d) manage his/her **ego** for his/her own benefit.

These four personality factors reflect people's major urges to think, feel, and behave in certain ways:

- **Instincts** drive many of our urges starting from the basic urge for sex all the way to the complex urge for spirituality. This factor reflects the *inner self* of a person.
- **Model** drives our urges to socialize and adapt. This factor reflects the *social orientation* of a person and his/her need for acceptance.
- **Ego** drives our urges to defend ourselves and to push our desires on others. This factor reflects the *object orienta-*

tion of a person, i.e., greed and a need to succeed in acquiring objects or dominating them.

- **Logic** drives our urges for decision making and planning. It reflects our ability to use our brain and reason. This factor reflects the *goal orientation* of a person.

A combination of above four factors makes up a person's personality. Accordingly, the intensity of each factor in the mix makes his/her personality unique.

A person with a *rather perfect* personality can make the best use of his/her instincts, has great common sense, knows how best to adapt to the environment, and applies his/her Ego in the most *effective manner*. 'Effective Manner' demands that this person's objectives are humanistic and not merely selfish. Many people can use their Ego and Model effectively for personal benefit only, e.g., our haughty politicians who manipulate the public for their own and their sponsors' benefits. However, a rather perfect personality must acquire certain qualities that can make the person a better human being overall.

Therefore, it becomes clear that hardly anybody has a perfect, balanced personality. We have our unique personalities, which reflect our strengths and weaknesses in terms of the personality factors that we have inherited genetically or acquired in society. For example, a person with higher Model tendency is mostly emphasizing on socializing and adaptation, whereas a person with high Ego tendency is too selfish and mostly object oriented. A person could be considered normal, and not perfect, when s/he makes a rather balanced use of all his/her personality factors. Alas, most of us do not qualify even as a normal person due to our insecurities, quirks, and inadequate use of instincts and logic. We are mostly Model and Ego driven, which means we have high social and object orientations, and are trapped in our obsessions for love, greed, and egoism.

Approximate ratings for human personalities, along the above noted four factors, are offered in the following pages based on a simple mechanism developed by the author. This mechanism provides a chance for making some tentative estimates of gender and average personality ratings in modern societies. For interested readers and scholars, the background for these ratings, including a personality chart, is provided at the end of the book in the References.

Overall, the personality ratings offered in this book suggest that an average human in a modern society is only slightly driven by instincts (about 20% of all his/her instinctual capacities), he/she knows how to adapt to his/her environment by using his Model (on about 70% of occasions), and he/she is highly self-centred and object-oriented (in about 80% of his/her dealings with people), and he/she benefits from logic and common sense to some extent (about 30% of his/her total potential). Thus, using the above noted percentages, we can say that an overall personality rating for humans is (20,70,80,30), which reflects their capacity for using their instincts, model, ego, and logic respectively. This rating is obviously too far off the ideal personality that can be imagined for a relatively perfect personality.

Gender Personality Ratings

Now, the fun part!

Men and women with all types of personality ratings are found anywhere on the wide personality spectrum (i.e. in the rectangle shown in the Chart in References). However, it is probably safe to suggest the average ratings of (30,80,70,20) and (10,60,90,40) for women and men respectively. These two ratings are shown as 'Women' and 'Men' in the Chart.

These ratings reflect that women are depending more (compared to men) on their instincts in their decisions and actions (30% for women versus 10% for men). On the other hand, men depend more on their logic (20% for women versus 40% for men). Women's intuitiveness helps them in many ways as explained in this book. Mainly, it makes them more capable of applying their Model to their advantage in a natural way and adapt easier in social settings. Model makes them more charming than men (80% for women versus 60% for men). In addition, it helps them to rebound after a relationship breakdown much better and faster. Use of their Instincts and Model also makes women more assertive and decisive. They also are better equipped to bond together more naturally and deeply than men do. Men are weaker in all these respects. Men are more aggressive because they are more Ego oriented than women (70% for women versus 90% for men).

For comparison, gender ratings for four personality factors are laid side by side, according to the level (percentage) of Instincts, Model, Ego, and Logic:

	Instincts	Model	Ego	Logic

Women : (30,80,70,20)
Men   : (10,60,90,40)
Humans: (20,70,80,30)

Gender differences in terms of people's use of their four personality factors appear not significant on the surface, yet even these minor differences are affecting gender qualities and attitude noticeably. Even one percent variation in any single personality factor, e.g., use of Ego, makes a big difference in a person's perceptions and behaviour. The symptoms and effects are not only vivid during our personal contacts, but also lead to major relationship conundrums and the rise in divorce rate. Of course, gender differences account only for a portion of a person's personality. Family genetics and rearing environment affect people's personality much deeper than any other factor, including human hormones.

On the other hand, it seems most likely that gender differences will increase every decade, as culture and people's personal tendencies increase in line with their higher neediness and obsession for individualism. Social setting and people's shallow lifestyles affect the formation of people's unique personalities. Thus, gender differences would widen every decade and relationship conflicts increase too. Of course, everybody would still hold all the four main dimensions of personality attributes, especially Ego, which its share would most likely continue to rise in both genders. Everybody is getting more self-centred and phony every year. Besides the effect of more egoism on culture and its repercussions for relationships, the symptoms of new developments (e.g., more egoism) would manifest in different ways in genders.

CHAPTER TWO
Gender Personality Attributes

PERSONALITY develops according to people's genetics, rearing environment, outlook, gender, and life experiences. Accordingly, personality attributes are often unique qualities that help people manage their lives, be assertive, and defend themselves. Furthermore, these personal qualities could help couples in their relationships, if they appreciated the values of their gender differences to create higher efficiency through cooperation. In fact, these qualities are often so nicely complementary, as if God or evolution has designed them artfully just for couples' welfare through teamwork. Yet, nowadays, couples sabotage nature's clever scheme. They do not know how to mix their gender qualities to increase synergy in their relationships. Our modern mentality seems to be ruining the effect of natural evolution that aids all creatures. We refuse to grasp and enjoy God's divine intention for making genders different! Instead, everybody insists on propagating some presumed perceptions of equality and doing the same types of activities with intense competition. Thus, instead of benefiting their qualities, couples worry about equality. Consequently, all the inherent qualities in one's personality often turn into quirks and inconveniences for others, e.g., when confidence turns into cockiness.

Nevertheless, five fundamental facts about gender qualities and quirks are important to consider throughout our discussions in this book:

1. People have much more common traits and quirks than they have differences. Genders have many common personality attributes, such as ambition, greed, and a big host of crooked personal needs like the ones discussed in Chapter Eight. The amount of relationship frictions caused by those common needs and traits of people, regardless of their gender, is probably as much as it is caused by gender differences.

2. Although genders' high qualities and symptoms irritate the opposite gender, without such disparity they would have tortured each other and ruined their relationships even more. Just imagine both genders being equally decisive and active based on their intuitions, or were both passive. Not only more frictions would have erupted all the time between partners, but also their whole life outcome would have become even more risky without at least some basic checks and balances that the present gender differences impose on relationships.

3. Each gender quality and its symptoms are related to the other personality attributes (qualities and symptoms) for that gender. For example, men's passivity is the outcome of their cautious mind, loose nature, realism, poor identity, etc. Thus, people cannot change their personality attributes readily even if they agreed they were destructive for them or their relationships.

4. The challenge for couples is to learn to somehow apply their conflicting gender qualities to their advantage in order to relate more effectively and create synergy in their relationships. This objective should eventually feel natural and logical to them. Then they can find means of doing it through compromise and teamwork by respecting their conflicting qualities wisely instead of remaining self-centred and dogmatic about their gender identities and whimsical ideals.

5. Accordingly, the first step to move toward this sacred objective is for people and society to revamp their mentalities about the purposes and potentials of relationships and become rather realistic for reaching a more practical end.

Obviously, we cannot change the course of history and the effect of vast social changes. Most likely, we can never benefit from the full potentials of gender differences within the growing culture either. However, we might be able to develop at least a more productive perspective about gender differences to improve our relationships somewhat. Anyhow, this book's primary purpose of studying gender differences and personality attributes is to suggest a list of both qualities and quirks that seem more attributable to one gender in general. Then, we might eventually learn to use that information for at least some moderate benefits in our relationships.

Sometimes, separating gender qualities from quirks becomes only a matter of personal taste and opinion, maybe even due to our mood swings. Normally, only our own personal defects and misperceptions make other people's qualities appear devilish to us or some of their quirks feel normal or even useful. Our misperceptions also affect our relationships adversely due to the way we all view and react to our partners and their intentions and perceive their qualities as quirks. Merely our shallow mentalities and decision criteria make us misjudge the real value of our partners and relationships. Thus, we react positively or negatively to our partners' qualities and quirks improperly.

Cultural perceptions of gender qualities, inequalities, and quirks add to the mayhem as well. Many of our newer values are erroneous and misleading too often without partners' intention to be so negative and antagonistic. Nevertheless, the outcome of these gender differences in marital relationships is of interest in this book and thus discussed only to help us improve our relationships. As a starting point, in fact, we should initially consider personality attributes mainly as personal and gender qualities, instead of defects or shortcomings that keep ruining our relationships. We just need to reassess our perspective of gender qualities and learn how they hinder partners' ability to relate.

Therefore, as the general structure of this book, gender qualities are emphasized in Part I, and gender quirks are further analysed in Part II. Even then, the point for discussing quirks is mostly for understanding the effect of gender differences and the nature of relationship conflicts caused by them, merely for revamping our mentality and helping our relationships. Accordingly, Part III's discussions are also for increasing couples' awareness and sensitivity in their relationship by learning more about the nature of gender quarrel that result mostly from genders' unique quirks and qualities.

As noted in the previous Chapter, men and women are found everywhere on the Personality Chart with large variations in terms of their personality attributes. The proportions of each personality factor used (regardless of the gender) vary among people quite noticeably too. Overall, however, all humans (both genders) use very similar levels of personality factors. Merely the minor differences in the use of the four personality factors (i.e., instincts, logic, model, and ego) account for the rather vast gender differences that cause relationship hurdles.

If we draw the four personality factors suggested in the last chapter on a scale, men and women positions in terms of using personality factors looks as shown below:

Humans

Instincts	Model	l	Ego	Logic

Women   **Men**

This scale shows the percentages of personality factors that men and women use (on the average) in their interactions:

Personality Factors	Women	Men	Humans
Instincts	30%	10%	20%
Model	80%	60%	70%
Ego	70%	90%	80%
Logic	20%	40%	30%

The above ratings reflect humans' natural (instinctual) and acquired urges in general, according to the emerging social circumstances, which lead to some unique personality attributes and noticeable gender differences.

Women are closest to Model and the furthest away from Logic. Conversely, men are closest to Ego and the furthest away from Instincts. That is, while both genders benefit from all personality factors almost equally, men are just a bit more egotistical and logical, compared with women, who are somewhat more social (Model) and intuitive than men. The overall average between the genders provides the rating for Humans—somewhere between the Women and Men points.

Gender Qualities

We have all noticed and wondered about some gender differences (qualities) like the ones shown below.

Gender Differences (Qualities)

Women	Men
1. Decisive	1. Cautious
2. Active	2. Passive
3. Neat and organized	3. Loose/Natural
4. Seek independence	4. Seek dependence
5. Optimistic in general	5. Realistic in general
6. Strong identity	6. Poor identity
7. Maternal	7. Creative
8. Seek love	8. Low trust in love
9. High MLove	9. Low MLove
10. Adventurous/Choosy	10. Preoccupied

These gender qualities reflect genders' peculiar views of life and social setting in the new era. They are merely the outcome of minor gender differences in the percentages of personality factors (e.g., instincts, model, ego, logic) that people use. Furthermore, they are obviously affected by culture and society and it changes in time. Therefore, the list of gender qualities, as well as their symptoms, are relevant mostly for the present era, e.g., while women are too keen to assert their independence and enforce equality. The other important point is that these personality attributes are in fact *qualities* that help each gender and every person individually, but they could also become handy if couples learn how to combine these qualities and create synergy in their relationships.

People's personality attributes (qualities) appear in their attitudes and thoughts both positively and negatively, e.g., in the form of originality, spite, jealousy, etc. These reaction or outcome of personality attributes are referred to as 'symptoms' in this book and discussed in the next chapter. Studying these widespread symptoms in society is also helpful for measuring the significance of gender differences, and vice versa. These symptoms best demonstrate the outcome of gender contacts and frictions. For example, we might be interested to know whether one gender is spiteful more than the other based on the prevalent symptoms of genders' attitude and mentality in the new era.

Nevertheless, the above noted unique gender qualities and their symptoms seem to have major practical implications in daily life, gender interactions, and relationships' health.

List of Women's Qualities

Women's main qualities (personality attributes) affect their ways of thinking, feeling and behaving somewhat uniquely as discussed in the following:

1. Even the slightly better use of their instincts, gives women a higher degree of intuitiveness compared to men.
2. In return, their higher intuitiveness, make women more decisive than men.
3. As an exception, however, women are less decisive than men regarding their careers. On the other hand, they are more decisive about finding happiness and a lifestyle akin to their fantastical life outlook. Accordingly, while less

committed to their careers than men, they are more adventurous about life itself.

4. With higher instinctual tendency and natural handling of Model, women are satiated with all three types of love, i.e., ELove, MLove, and SLove. Furthermore, they can maintain a practical balance among these three types of love better than men can.

   The three types of love are explained in full in other books in these series. In a nutshell, the following definitions are used in the remainder of this book: (These definitions are posted at the end of the book in References, too, for ease of access when necessary.)

   • SLove (selfless love) is the purest kind of love we feel toward our children, Nature, and possibly for our artistic creations. We could also say that S stands for 'Serving.' With SLove, we Serve (give) love Selflessly.

   • ELove (egotistic love) reflects our selfish need for love and attention and is mostly a reflection of insecurity. Alternately, E could stand for 'Expecting.' With ELove, we Expect (demand) love Egotistically.

   • MLove (model love) is the tactful expressions of love to show compassion and cope with social etiquette. Alternately, M could stand for 'Moderating.' With MLove, we try to Moderate our relationships Modestly accordingly to a tactful Model.

5. Higher instinctual urges have also given women higher emotional tendencies and a higher Model aptitude to adapt and fit better in society.

6. The combination of their higher Model and decisiveness enable and encourage women to be more active in social settings, relationships, and family life. They also like to organize and manage things quickly and move on.

7. Women have traditionally taken less risks as they have felt obliged to take care of their offspring. Now, an inner conflict arises for women who like to be active, take more risks, and be adventurous, but feel their instinctual need to protect their offspring by averting risks and being less active about their careers.

8. Consequently, nowadays, men and women behave differently outside and inside the house. While women are somewhat less competitive and more passive at work, they are quite competitive and active (in charge) at home as part of their inherent nature, but also for compensating their work-related mindset. Men do the same in the opposite direction. These differences are obviously related to gender differences in terms of social goals and values, too, e.g., women's views of career and family as explained in note # 3 above.

9. Women have a high tendency (bordering obsession) for the cleanliness and tidiness of their households. This tendency is most likely the outcome of several personality attributes mixing, including a high desire for likeability and sociability, action orientation, maternal sensibility, and decisiveness.

10. Women seek more independence in order to assert their identity in modern society after many years of inequity, inequality, and oppression by men. However, inherently, they need dependence on a partner at least for emotional support more than ever.

11. Women are more optimistic about life and love. They live longer perhaps because of their positive attitude too. (Although the stress from working outside the house and love deprivation would most likely reduce women's life expectancy in the years to come.) Women's positive attitude helps them rebound faster than men after a separation,

since they keep hoping for good things and love coming their ways soon.

12. Women have been able to portray a strong identity for themselves. They know what they want and are learning fast how to get it. They are focused and determined. This feels rather natural and easy for them because they must only focus on their past deprivation, such as equality and independence. Now, all they must do is to find the ways of getting those seemingly precious things.

13. Women's maternal instincts and sensitivity are much stronger than men due to genetics, hormones, etc.

14. Women seek love more actively due to their instinctual and emotional tendencies. They also seem to have a higher need for things including fashion, art, and household decorations. Women's search for love and things appear deep and instinctual, as if these needs were totally authentic and heartfelt—often even reaching the level of obsession. This personality attribute is again in line with their higher need for likeability and sociability.

15. The overall effect of the gender differences noted above supports the observation that women are more romantic and needy for a companion despite their efforts to appear independent, decisive, and needless. At least, they are more open about their search for love than men are. They live in a world of fantasy with many dreams, especially about love and the possibility of finding a prince.

16. As noted above, due to their high Model, women have a higher MLove as well. This means that they express their feelings easier and more masterfully. This ability increases their charm and chances of fulfilling their needs much better. In a way, one might say that women are better equipped to manipulate men.

17. Women are more adventurous, at least mentally, in the sense that they seek variety and pleasures more actively to express themselves and enjoy life. Accordingly, they are choosy in terms of things they like to do and people they befriend, while remain sociable in general very well too.
18. Women like and seek new challenges due to their active nature, but also for capturing a higher sense of life and happiness.

A great proof of all the above qualities, especially item #2 about women's decisiveness, is evident in the fact that women initiate marital separations in North America in about 70% of the cases. This statistics probably applies to Europe and all other countries where women have the right to ask for divorce. This is the most important life decision in normal conditions due to so many reasons explained in the author's other books, including *Marriage and Divorce Hardships*. Yet, for women the decision to ask for separation feels rather easy, necessary, or natural in our current culture.

List of Men's Qualities

Men's main qualities (personality attributes) affect their ways of thinking, feeling and behaving somewhat uniquely, too, as discussed in the following:

1. Men are slightly more dependent on their logic compared with women who are more intuitive.
2. Even this little difference in the use of logic makes men appear different (mostly slow) in terms of making decision.

3. Accordingly, men are hesitant to draw conclusions and make decisions before they have spent enough time to review all the alternatives. Therefore, they appear rather passive.

4. Men are somewhat looser and more natural about daily life routines, including cleanliness and tidiness.

5. Men seek dependence, but need more independence. They have always sought dependence on a partner for sex, companionship, and support in maintaining a household. They are simply too lazy and incompetent in keeping the household shipshape.

6. Men are more realistic about life and love because they make better use of past information due to their logical tendencies. They lose hope rather fast in order to reach stability and a state of contentment.

7. At this point, the shock and confusion are keeping men divided, numb, and unorganized about their identity in the new culture. Due to their lower intuition and lower Model, they have not been able to understand the new culture introduced by women. They have been somewhat caught off-guard and they have not yet been able to formulate a new identity for themselves to satisfy women's needs without losing even more of their own identity.

8. Higher logical tendencies of men have led to their higher analytical ability, creativity, and philosophizing during the mankind history. Within this environment, men have acquired a higher Ego aptitude and become more arrogant.

9. Their higher Ego and analytical tendency goad men to become rather passive, isolated, and to strive for self-actualization.

10. Relative to women, men's need for love and things appear to be moderate and mostly for feeding their Ego (power)

and for attracting women anyway. Of course, men's Ego and greed goad them to make more money to prove themselves. Like all other males in the animal kingdom, men fight, compete, and try to fulfil women's needs, mostly for reaping the rewards of their company and feeding their own Ego.

11. Men's obsessions relate more to power, pleasure, and creativity instead of love and objects per se. Yet, due to their passive attitude about love, and higher deprivation of love, men are inherently more vulnerable emotionally.

12. Men have less faith in love due to their logical orientation, and because they apply the prevalent information about relationship failures more analytically. In the older cultures, love had much less value for men, and that mentality has been passed on to men in the new generations largely as well. They have always been less romantic, anyway, and thus the effect of the new culture and the movies about romance and love has been lesser on men than it has been on women.

13. Yet, men are equally sensitive and very much emotional, if not more than women are in many instances. Their lack of trust in love and their inability, or the lack of opportunity, to express their emotions reduce their ability to relate to their partners, which then leads to deep inner conflicts for them too.

14. Men's high Ego, and low Model, curtails their ability to seek love as openly as they need. They are more practical and realize soon that finding a princess is merely a myth. However, as noted above, they are more vulnerable emotionally.

15. Overall, men seem preoccupied with immediate issues and certain primary features of life, compared to women who

desire to be involved with more activities and new adventures.

16. Accordingly, men are happier (than women) with the status quo and the way things are instead of doing new stuff just for the heck of it.

Note: While the above 18 and 16 qualities enumerated for women and men relate more directly to that particular group, they also reflect on the opposite gender's personality attribute indirectly. For example, when we consider women more decisive, it implies that men are less decisive compared to women.

The point made at the end of the last section about women's tendency (in 70% of cases) to request for separation confirms the points made above about men's qualities as well, especially their passivity and indecisiveness.

CHAPTER THREE
Personality Symptoms

ALL those unique and useful personality attributes for men and women listed in the previous chapter make them think, feel, and behave in creative and emotional ways. They become who they are in the form they present themselves to others, but also in terms of reacting to other people's attitude, especially in their family relationships. Their inner conflicts, life experiences, and personal qualities make their thoughts and behaviours appear bizarre to others. Therefore, many of our personal qualities turn into, or are perceived as, quirks.

Accordingly, pressure mounts in relationships because partners are annoyed by each other's quirks instead of appreciating each other's qualities. Even worse, couples do not know how to combine their qualities and personality attributes in order to relate and work together in a teamwork environment. Thus, the symptoms of gender differences manifest in a destructive form. All those personal qualities in fact begin to clash and relationship conflicts arise at so many levels. Using the men's and women's lists of personality attributes in the last chapter, we can see how those qualities are suddenly envisioned and treated as idiosyncrasies. The list of *symptoms* related to each of the qualities listed for men and women, as shown in the following pages, show how every one of those personality attributes (qualities) turn into sources of conflict and headaches in relationships.

By the way, the 'Qualities' and 'Symptoms' listed in the following pages for women and men must be viewed as general tendencies and not scientific notions. It is impossible to generalize easily in social sciences, especially about human behaviour and personality. The gender tendencies and differences noted here are by no means complete either. They are only examples of the most common observations about genders' interactions and communications. With this disclaimer, the assertions in this book are in line with the author's and other scholars' general experiments and observations. They are presented in the same order of the ten qualities listed below. Yet, some points may be repeated when they apply to more than one item on the list. All the discussions in this book about gender differences are also based on this chapter's general assumptions and conclusions.

Women's Personality

Women show the following distinct qualities and symptoms:

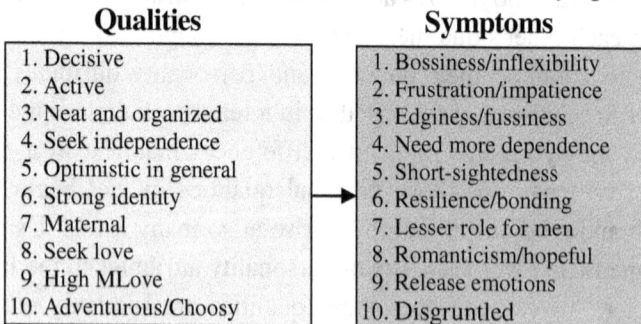

Qualities	Symptoms
1. Decisive	1. Bossiness/inflexibility
2. Active	2. Frustration/impatience
3. Neat and organized	3. Edginess/fussiness
4. Seek independence	4. Need more dependence
5. Optimistic in general	5. Short-sightedness
6. Strong identity	6. Resilience/bonding
7. Maternal	7. Lesser role for men
8. Seek love	8. Romanticism/hopeful
9. High MLove	9. Release emotions
10. Adventurous/Choosy	10. Disgruntled

1. The effect of women's decisiveness is that they appear bossy and inflexible with their viewpoints. Their intuitiveness makes women more certain about their conclusions and thus become less flexible. They are bossy and rigid also because they are frustrated with their procrastinating husbands. Often, however, their inflexibility is perceived by men as a sign of insensitivity. The perceived low sensitivity is, of course, not contradictory to the fact that women are usually better in expressing their emotions with their higher Model and MLove when necessary.

   In fact, women's occasional show or appearance of insensitivity may come as a surprise and contradictory to their attitude of oversensitivity noted in the following item # 2. However, these seemingly personality contradictions are the realities that make women too complex and mysterious.

2. Higher instinctual urges and keener perceptions of life have made women sensitive and often oversensitive to the point of overreacting to simplest inconvenience and low attention. Women's oversensitivity causes more inner conflict and concern for them when men are becoming more preoccupied and less sensitive in general.

3. Women's active mindset and personality make them impatient and frustrated when their plans and wishes do not proceed as fast or satisfactory to them. This situation is another factor for becoming bossy to get things going.

4. The effect of women's obsession for cleanliness and tidiness is that women come across as uptight and fussy. Their tendency to depend so much on their intuition also contributes to their edginess.

5. Women's struggle to gain and show their independence jeopardize their inherent need for dependence. Independ-

ence is obviously synonymous with needlessness. So, the more women play the role of needless partners, the more men find themselves alienated in terms of helping women with their dependency need. Many reasons exist for this debilitating condition. However, one obvious reason is that, as civilized people, we try to help someone or interfere in his/her affairs only when he/she asks for help. It feels awkward to interfere with the affairs of a spouse who insists on being needless at so many levels all the time. Unfortunately, partners are getting confused about 'when' to provide or seek help, especially emotional support. Misperceptions and misinterpretations about help sought or provided are making couples both anxious and oversensitive about their relationships. The bottom line is that the women's need for dependence on a reliable partner is left increasingly unfulfilled. Meanwhile, their higher Model and emotional tendencies reinforce their need for dependence even more. The dilemma of dependence versus independence is discussed in more details in Chapter Eight due to its importance.

6. Neither gender has yet decided about a right balance between their dependence/independence needs, which they need in order to minimize their inner conflicts. In particular, they must balance their gender-oriented needs in order to communicate effectively with each other. At the same time, it is questionable whether the natural properties of genders would ever allow them reach a practical balance for their dependence and independence needs at the levels that are also acceptable to the other gender. This particular symptom of gender needs in the new era has vast implications for many other aspects of relationships nowadays, mainly because couples' reactions toward this imbalance

are too harsh and futile. As long as this imbalance prevails in personal lives of people and in terms of relating to one another in relationships, the matter would cause only further alienation and havoc in relationships.

7. Women's idealism and higher optimism in life makes them less concerned about the potential risks ahead. They seem to concentrate mostly on the near future, perhaps now. For example, they seem to show an obsession to own a house regardless of the financial justifications. Their shortsightedness is a symptom of over-optimism, which obviously make planning and risk management difficult in relationships.

8. Women's struggles and success in recent decades to define a proper identity for themselves have led to higher resilience and bonding among them. They have proven capable of supporting one another and bonding for their common objectives. They have developed many new techniques and games to achieve what they want and stay vigilant about the progress of their plans. They have learned to make money and be independent, and, of course, they are more optimistic about life in general too. To ensure their plans are not jeopardized, they have become calculating and assertive, and sometimes even aggressive. As a whole, women have developed a specific and concrete identity (or at least an image of it) for themselves and are bonding together to make sure this identity is promoted and protected. Women's cohesiveness and lower Ego have been helping them in reinforcing their new identity.

9. The stronger identity for women at the cost of men losing theirs would continue to damage relationships and both genders would suffer from this imbalance. Meanwhile, neither gender would find its true identity, because in the

final analyses they need each other to create their real identities.

10. The effect of women forcing their new progressive identity and men losing theirs would be interesting. One could argue that men's Ego would be curbed eventually, and thus a new relationship atmosphere might emerge. It is a possibility. However, the change, if any, would not be felt in this century for many reasons. First, Ego is an inherent trait for men built during a long history of humanity. So it cannot be undermined easily despite the women's attempt to tame it. It would take many decades to tone down men's egoism, if at all possible. Second, the force of Ego in men would not allow the existing situation, i.e., their loss of identity, continue for too long. Even the existing passive reactions by men could result in the emergence of new relationship approaches. Men are equally intelligent and maybe even capable of colluding, eventually, in order to reclaim some kind of identity for themselves. Nonetheless, both genders would realize the necessity of creating the needed balances and attitudes. Men's loss of identity is, thus, a temporary situation. A new identity for men would emerge eventually within a century or so. The question is how passive and submissive it would be!

11. A similar comment can be made about women's present Model tendency. With their new approach, they already seem (or pretend) to be gaining a great deal of Ego. If this continues, many of the above personality traits would no longer remain valid. They would erode naturally. Yet again, the reality is that women's instinctual tendencies are too deep to be drastically subdued by their attempt to create a man-like identity for themselves. They would always be the tender mother that nature has meant them to be, de-

spite the perceived image of their insensitivity on many occasions. Nonetheless, the existing state of transition would hopefully come to a practical equilibrium eventually. In that steady state, both genders have clear identities that lead to a higher synergy in relationships.

12. Women's powerful maternal urge pushes them not only in terms of seducing men for the ultimate purpose of procreation, but also finding a lesser value in men afterward. Nature is possibly making women more demanding and commanding to take care of the whole family efficiently. Therefore, they treat men like another child. They keep nagging and pushing them away into an emotional standby, at least temporarily. To women, babies are their ultimate creations that satisfy their need for self-actualization and dependence largely. Thus, children become the centre of their focus. Although women would continue to have a strong need for dependency on men (mostly for socializing and ELove), this urge is somewhat dampened, at least while their children keep them busy and while they know that their faithful husbands are still around at a safe distance.

13. Women's natural (historical) tendency to treat men like another child might have contributed a lot to men's seclusion. They became more self-reliant and developed a higher need for self-actualization, creativity, and Ego.

14. Conversely, women became more Model oriented to support one another and their offspring with lesser need for males. On the other hand, men's perception of (and frustration about) women's insensitivity toward them might have contributed to men's seclusion and aggressiveness toward women.

15. Women's belief and obsession to find love make them too romantic and hopeful at the cost of losing their chance of getting a more realistic perspective of relationships in the new era. They overestimate men's ability to deal with this new and rather fanciful expectation.

16. As noted before, women encourage one another to be assertive with their husbands and leave them if they cannot respond to their desires. The question here is women's motives. Do they provoke one another out of kindness, malice, rivalry, jealousy, ignorance, or a combination of these incentives? A cynical viewpoint is that they often do it to screw up one another intentionally, either for personal reasons or to promote women's presumed identity. The jury is out on this one. Yet, some good explanations might exist for doing it for their own benefit and not necessarily out of kindness. Getting into these discussions is beyond the purpose of this book, however. Nonetheless, women believe that by propagating a low-tolerance attitude, they would enforce their identity and feminism and keep their husbands under control. This mentality might backfire and deteriorate the chances of harmony in relationships even further.

17. Overall, women have a higher tendency for jealousy and rivalry, despite their high aptitude for bonding. In particular, they are very competitive amongst themselves in terms of objects and the passion they seek from their husbands or other men. They also compete amongst themselves in terms of pushing their identity. They struggle to demonstrate their individuality and dominance in their relationships in order to excel other women on these factors. All these competitions infect their relationships.

18. The human hormones and their cyclical changes impact genders' brain activities differently. Especially women are more susceptible to depression, anxiety, and mood swings due to hormonal changes during maternity, menstrual cycle, and menopause.

19. The genders' distinct 'brain functions' make them react to various life conditions and stress quite differently. For example, the cortisol level, which measures stress intensity, is typically two times higher in women compared with men. This is due to the way women perceive pain much deeper and the way they must go about calming themselves.

20. While men try to deal with their stress by solving a typical problem or ignoring it altogether, women need to talk about their problems. The chance to talk releases serotonin in their brains that calms their limbic system. There are also twice as many women on antidepressants as men based on recent statistics.

21. In all, hormones usually make women more decisive and optimistic about life, and thus they set high expectations for their relationships. Along with new slogans and approaches in society, women are nowadays more idealistic and seek love and happiness more obsessively, too, which then lead to their higher depression and uptightness. Hormones have also increased women's ability to bond and be outgoing.

22. Women are bearing a great deal more inner conflicts than men because their new identity and social role do not coincide with their instinctual, maternal, and romantic tendencies. In particular, women have a tougher time (and more inner conflicts) for creating a balance between their opposing needs for dependence and inde-

pendence. The symptoms of women's high inner conflicts appear in their higher edginess and frustration,
which naturally lead to various types of relationship
conflicts too.

All the above symptoms clash with the symptoms of men's
personality attributes (qualities), as discussed in the next section, and together they cause havoc in relationships, although
both genders try to do their best to deal with these symptoms.

Men's Personality

Men's personality becomes distinctive by the following qualities and symptoms:

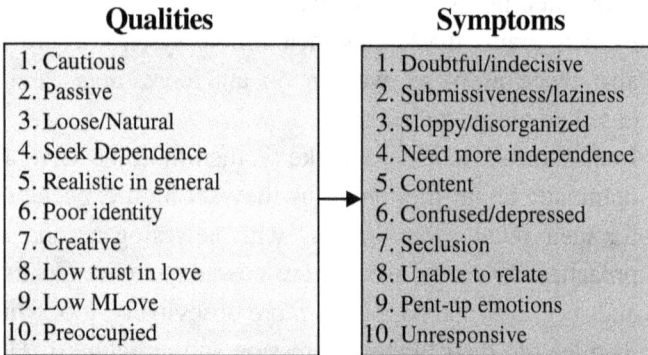

Qualities	Symptoms
1. Cautious	1. Doubtful/indecisive
2. Passive	2. Submissiveness/laziness
3. Loose/Natural	3. Sloppy/disorganized
4. Seek Dependence	4. Need more independence
5. Realistic in general	5. Content
6. Poor identity	6. Confused/depressed
7. Creative	7. Seclusion
8. Low trust in love	8. Unable to relate
9. Low MLove	9. Pent-up emotions
10. Preoccupied	10. Unresponsive

1. The symptoms of men's cautious and contemplation for
   making decisions portrays them as indecisive and lacking
   spontaneity.
2. Of course, men are trying to be practical by disallowing
   spontaneity affect their decisions and cause tragedy. Some
   men actually realize their partial responsibility for their
   wives' anxiety (due to men's indecisiveness) and thus try

to make up for it by patience and adaptation. That is, to make up for their indecisiveness, they learn to absorb and tolerate their partners' reactions, including their bossiness. Thus, the level of men's submissiveness has been increasing in recent decades.

3. Contrary to women, who are intuitively decisive, men must be forced into making a decision by timelines, business obligations, desperation, etc. Their indecisiveness manifest in the way they hesitate in choosing and proposing to a woman too. Women usually make a decision about the suitability of a man rather quickly.

4. The effect of men's tendencies toward logic, analysis, creativity, and philosophizing has made them feel and appear rather self-absorbed and uncaring.

5. Men's excess Ego over Model ultimately turns them more inwardly and inactive in their relationships too. They must try hard to adapt themselves to this environment in order to minimize the amount of family clashes.

6. Men's passivity portrays them as lazy and submissive. Their passivity is then further reinforced and proven when they eventually let their wives run the family affairs, mostly because they (men) are actually lazy, even for arguments or confrontations.

7. Although men are less instinctual than women are in general, they seem more loose and natural in terms of their attitude and they are more inclined to live in the wilderness, rather inhibited. Accordingly, they acquire a different taste and priority for life than women do. In particular, the symptoms of their life priorities erupt in the way they consider cleanliness and tidiness a waste of their precious time. Yet, they can easily waste that time on odd hobbies, watching sports, or drinking beer.

8. The effect of their loose attitude and easygoing is that men come across as too careless and sloppy about issues that their wives give much higher priority to, mainly in terms of household appearance and cleanliness.

9. Men's search for dependence on a companion is mostly a symptom of their inherent need for independence and freedom. They wish to rely on their wives to manage the mundane family affairs and household, so that they can attend to the supposedly more immediate affairs outside the house. However, their need for dependence remains even more deprived nowadays as women insist on their independence and thus reduce the supply of reliable and consistent source of support for men. Men have a hard time to fulfil this objective. Thus, they seek dependence even more desperately—almost at the same level that women seek more independence.

However, men, by nature and their higher Ego, need more independence psychologically. They like to be left alone to spend time on their own contemplations, creating, and feeding their Ego. Therefore, men seek dependence (by looking for a companion) mainly for getting the opportunity of fulfilling their need for independence. In the older times, men got the dependence they sought rather easily. Thus, they could fulfil their need for independence easier too. However, they have now lost the means of satisfying both their dependence and independence needs. Nowadays, they must pay a high price to obtain the dependence they seek in a companion. The price is paid in the form of giving up more and more of their independence, which they crave instinctually and had always enjoyed easily in the past. The amount of independence they must forgo to gain a relative dependence often seems out of proportion (to them at least) and thus they are losing a chunk of their identities.

A reasonable question based on the above discussions is, 'Why men and women have difficulty relating to one another when their natural needs are indeed so nicely complementary?' Since both women and men *need* more dependence, why cannot they just fulfil each other's exact needs, while they balance their needs for independence more civilly too? The answer is that both genders want and demand both dependence and independence simultaneously and rather erratically. Although each gender *needs* something, it *seeks* a different thing more prominently. Their real needs (for dependence and independence) are exactly opposite to what they *seek* and express openly. They just hide their natural needs from each other. The dilemma of dependence versus independence is discussed in more details in Chapter Eight due to its importance.

10. Since both genders have difficulty defining their needs for dependence and independence personally and in terms setting a balance for their relationships, they can neither satisfy their personal goals, nor create the right kind of atmosphere for teamwork and synergy.

11. The effect of men's higher tendency to remain realistic about life's promises and traps, along with their doubtfulness, goads them to strive for a state of relative stability and contentment, often through submissiveness around their family at least, while saving their energy to fight outside the house on more immediate issues.

12. Contrary to women who have succeeded in defining a kind of identity for themselves, men's inability to develop an identity has confused and depressed them. Men's higher Ego prevents them from organizing their thoughts

and finding common grounds. They are passive and lazy about this matter too, of course. They have so far not taken women's drive for a new identity seriously enough either. They naively imagined that the situation was under control. Now, however, they must forgo a lot of their independence to acquire the dependence they seek in a companion. They do not know how to develop a new identity to cope with the emerging environment. Instead, they are becoming more submissive and passive. Therefore, the effect of this situation is that men are becoming further isolated and frustrated with their relationships. Women are also frustrated but for different reasons, mainly men's passivity.

13. Men's lower sense of maternity and limited involvement with child rearing continue to keep their role secondary to women's at best.

14. Men's lower sensitivity, due a bit higher logical tendency, realism, and mistrust in love, has led to their general scepticism about love, and thus lower MLove and a capacity to relate in relationships.

15. The effect of men's self-absorption and low Model curtails their ability to seek love as openly as they need it. Thus, their real emotions dampen, while they remain emotionally more vulnerable than women who can express and seek MLove more proactively.

16. Men's lower Model and MLove and pent-up emotions lead to frustration and aggression, especially when they insist on pushing logic while their wives are seeking more support and affection.

17. At the same time, men end up being preoccupied due to their sense of obligation, desperation, and Ego. Thus, they

are, or appear, rather unresponsive to the high demands of their wives for more attention at so many levels.

18. In line with note # 22 (page 35) about women's rising inner conflicts, men's inner conflicts are heightening, too, due to their loss of identity and the vagueness of their roles in family. However, their inner conflict symptoms are more moderate due to their passivity, pragmatism, and confusion.

The above rudimentary observations about gender differences have been made based on the list of gender qualities and symptoms suggested in this chapter, as well as the author's understanding of studies about human hormones. These observations also signify and verify the emergence of a peculiar trend in relationships, mostly in terms of our new approach toward sexuality and its potential outcome. In addition, they reflect women's higher optimism about life and the possibility of finding real love regardless of their age and their past negative experiences. Their optimism goads them to live in their fantasy world and keep looking for romance and beautiful things. Furthermore, they are very active nowadays in encouraging one another to seek perfection, love, independence and individuality. They encourage and support one another to leave their relationships when they cannot give them all the things and compassion they believe they deserve. They naively assume, all along, that men are psychologically capable of delivering all those things and compassion. Therefore, when they do not, it must be out of spite and stupidity.

On the other hand, men are more practical and give up on the idea of finding the perfect mate. Thus, they try to be a little more tolerant and accept mediocre relationships longer. Their minds are preoccupied with more immediate responsibilities or silly hobbies like sports. Their Ego and passivity, of course, cause relationship conflicts. However, the bottom line is that men cannot change themselves too much, not enough for the liking of women. Accordingly, couples face undue conflicts and separations. Women in particular keep saying that life is too short and you live only once. Therefore, they keep chasing their fantasy about men who can fulfil their dreams. They do not take notice that, while wasting their lives in search of acceptable men (if not ideal ones), they might be depriving themselves from the simple privileges of companionship and accomplishing some basic objectives that two people can attain better together if they stopped arguing too much about irresolvable gender differences and relationship issues. Thus, more loneliness and depression are emerging in society, while women keep searching for their imaginary mates, and men are becoming more sceptical about getting into relationships.

PART II

Gender Quirks

CHAPTER FOUR
General Quirks

HUMANS have a large variety of eccentricities and quirks that make them unique, interesting, impure, and evil too often. Many variables cause these flaws, including genetics and rearing environment. Especially, social values and teachings vastly affect our ways of thinking, feeling, and behaving. Then our efforts to build families scramble our emotions even deeper and cause mayhem in our relationships. Hence, the fast rising frictions and disharmony in modern relationships.

The main objective in Part II is to create an outline of general obstacles that gender differences impose on relationships. We like to know about the effects of gender symptoms and how they actually turn into real or perceived quirks and hinder couples' ability to relate. Some of the *general* quirks in relationships are discussed in this chapter, while the next two chapters will focus on each gender's specific quirks. The existing social setting discussed in this chapter is the symptom of all the emerging gender differences, after all.

We cannot deny the simple fact that men and women perceive the world, set their life priorities, and make decisions differently. These differences widen in modern societies where self-worth, equality, and independence find very high value. In addition, humans' inherent Ego and low capacity for compromise fuel the gender gap and pose major obstacles for a smooth process of communication and teamwork in relationships. This mayhem will persist until couples' mindsets are hopefully aligned with the relationship needs within the next few decades.

Grasping the roots of relationship conundrums, caused by genders' qualities and quirks, and improving couples' mindsets are the main steps to improve the health of relationships. We should also realize that our present social setting is extremely conducive to widening gender differences, which would in turn cause more social mayhem, relationship conflicts, and personal disappointments. The bottom line is that couples must raise their awareness, and maybe revamp their mindsets, about human nature and gender differences that lead to conflicts and confrontations in relationships. Grasping and admitting to the following facts can raise our level of compassion and thus improve our relationships:

1. Humans' four personality factors (i.e., instincts, model, ego, and logic) build and reflect their unique qualities and quirks.
2. Although gender differences on use of these factors are not substantial, even those minor differences seem to lead to noticeable variations in terms of attitude, feeling, and thinking between women and men.
3. Each gender has a rather uniform way of interpreting the world and setting its life priorities according to the culture and prevalent social values.
4. Accordingly, each gender has some common *qualities* that make that group appear rather eccentric to the other gender.

5. The *symptoms* of genders' unique qualities could be, or may appear, positive or negative to others.

6. A large set of inner (psychological) and outer (socioeconomic) forces drives everybody to perceive the world and others uniquely. Thus, we often feel, think, and act rather oddly inadvertently. This awareness can increase both our personal tolerance and sympathy toward our partners.

7. Accordingly, gender differences affect people's motivations behind their actions and feelings too. For example, while both genders have equal sexual drives, they often have different motives for acting upon it. All these varied gender motivations are behind the weird gender symptoms, e.g., men's higher tendency for aggression or laziness, as noted in this book.

8. Women's natural superiority in creating and safeguarding their offspring appears to contribute to the fact that men lose their priority in relationships when children are born.

9. An outer force affecting relationships adversely without anyone's fault is that women are in a state of transition in terms of the progressive role they would like to play in society and relationships.

10. Women's new role in relationships is not understood even by the majority of women, let alone by men who are expected to not only know what the new format should be, but also respond positively too.

11. It would be an inherently difficult task, for men especially, to achieve the changes required in terms of gender roles, even in a timelier manner, even if they agreed to the changes women are asking of them.

12. Therefore, couples adhere to all kinds of destructive games, including manipulation, intimidation, and retaliation in hopes of enduring their relationships.

13. Couples want to set the tone of their relationships through power struggles, with the ultimate intentions of controlling their relationship and partners.

14. Within this confusing situation, all kinds of destructive aggressions by both men and women are convoluting the transition process. Instead of progress, we witness sabotages and retaliation, more games, more divorces, and family murder suicides.

15. The bottom line is that men have lost their identity (whatever it was, good or bad) and do not understand the sensibility of what is expected of them. And women are frustrated, too, because they cannot prove and enforce a new identity, which they believe they know what it is.

16. The result of the current confusion (about gender identities) is that partners finally get fed up with their struggles to convince each other logically. Therefore, they try to either dominate each other or resort to divorce.

17. It appears that, nowadays, too many people are always struggling to either find a companion or get rid of him/her.

18. Therefore, all our lives, we look for an imaginary idol to accept as our companion, or we try to rebuild (change) our partners to fit that image. Especially there is a trend out there to make men softer so that they can respond better to women's desires and perceptions of relationships

19. A special situation seems to have emerged: Due to men's passivity, women find it necessary to become aggressive in order to attain the assertiveness they need urgently.

20. Men and women are inherently incompatible in terms of nature. Therefore, partners' effort to find their compatible companion is mostly a shot in the dark anyway. And still the new relationship approaches and games make the job of finding our soul mate even tougher.

21. Peculiar signals that men and women send to one another by their attitudes and games are causing more distance between them. These role-playings and games are too difficult to understand or respond to.
22. The main cause of, and need for, these games is that couples do not grasp the reality and roots of gender difference and do not know how to deal with the natural symptoms of genders' personality attributes.
23. The games couples play to maintain the balance of power is an ongoing, exhausting process. Partners simply seem incapable of putting down their guards, to live and relate naturally.
24. Another problem is that even when a partner decides to stop playing games and behave naturally, he/she still cannot deal with his/her partner who is addicted to these relationship games.
25. The irony is that people always notice and criticize other people's games and phoniness, but not their own. Most often they are aware of the games and roles they are playing, but naively assume that people do not notice them. They believe in their playacting too much. Even worse, they think people are too simple or busy to see through them.
26. People play roles and games in order to maximize their relationships' chances for success. However, by doing so, they actually increase the chances of being rejected and resisted.
27. A frustrating situation in relationships develops when a partner insists on playing a role or game and the other partner is not falling for it.
28. Relationships fail because too many of partners' games keep clashing. The more games they play to cope with so-

cial and relationship issues, the more conflicts arise, which then lead to even more games.

29. Usually one partner starts a game with a special intention—mostly for handling the symptoms of his/her partner's personality attributes. Then the other partner starts his/her own game instead of playing along. The first partner is astonished that his/her game is detected and resisted. Therefore, they keep introducing more games until they are exhausted and angry.

30. People consider their acts of charming and manipulating others their absolute right and an effective tool, while they believe they are good at it too. So, when they fail, they just get too angry and nasty about it. All that charm suddenly turns into hostility and ruins even their basic capacity for relating.

31. The way people snub each other as a way of relating—to set the tone of their friendships and relationships—is funny.

32. Instead of expecting happiness from relationships, couples must realize that they should actually be willing to pay a big price for it. This is a major requirement they must accept before entering a relationship. Always a high price must be paid for the few fringe benefits of relationships.

33. People are ignoring the simple fact that retaliations cannot help them solve their relationship or personal problems.

34. In fact, anyone who is capable of retaliating harshly is inherently empty of compassion. In particular, it is quite silly when someone retaliates in order to force compassion in his or her relationships.

35. Love and anger are not compatible, and whoever uses anger to force (or keep) love is simply incapable of giving or receiving love.

36. With the advent of various dating facilities, people meet and learn about many candidates for dating. While this flexibility seems helpful to find a match, it also increases people's false hopes about the possibility of finding a qualified person soon. Therefore, they become too fussy and keep joggling a bunch of relationships. Meanwhile, people who are truly suitable for being in relationships are becoming scarcer too.

37. People keep multiple relationships because they are doubtful about the viability of any of them. In addition, it is more efficient to study a few prospect partners simultaneously, as it usually takes many years to get to know someone, if at all.

38. Having multiple relationships can also help a person rebound faster if one of his/her favourite relationships fails. He/she has other relationships to lean on at least temporarily. All these justifications sound reasonable, but what a weird world we have created.

39. Our hope to eventually find a soul mate is a naive incentive that stops us from making genuine efforts and commitments in a relationship or keeping our promises.

40. Under these tough circumstances, perhaps the best definition for a soul mate is, 'Someone we can get along with, finally!'

41. Another cause of the increasing mistrust in society and relationships is that people are aware of the games people play, including multiple dating. Therefore, it is hard for people to take their relationships seriously. Oddly, however, everybody is also too eager and hopeful to find a reliable companion as if s/he would arrive from another planet. People's struggle and optimism to find love, trust, and happiness are both admirable and depressing.

It is depressing because people seem to miss, or eager to ignore, the new realities of relationships.

42. Many people, especially women, take the flattery they receive a sign of their chances to find a better mate once they leave their present partners. Then after separation, they realize how they have been misled.

43. People, especially men, are enjoying the present situation with multiple dating and all, while they (mostly women) are getting more frustrated due to their failure to find a qualified partner and also facing men's increasing passivity.

44. People's reaction to the present relationship conditions is just to do more of the same, i.e., more games, multiple dating, lying and mistrust, more shallow relationships. Thus, the rising level of frustration in society.

45. The complexity of the relationship environment and our passivity about it are the reasons why it will take at least a century to find real solutions for relationships.

46. Many humble individuals are out there who could be in good relationships together if they were not deterred by their (often justified) paranoia about the state of relationships and their lack of trust in people.

47. People do not know how to be tactful or observe even simple etiquettes, but keep insisting on the purity of their soul.

48. While everybody is obsessed about finding his/her soul mate, the chance of it ever happening is slim. However, we all have difficulty accepting this fact, since we want to stay positive. Our romantic search for a soul mate is preventing us from perceiving relationships realistically and facing life as an independent person.

49. Couples' promises or commitments are not reliable. Especially, taking the phrase 'I love you' seriously, as a sign of commitment, is naïve.

50. People do not change unless they feel the need for it through years of meditation and self-awareness. Therefore, partners' retaliations and intimidations to change each other are just a reflection of their own naivety.
51. People, especially women, are nowadays too idealistic, ambitious, neurotic, and stressed out due to their new life-styles and fantasies.
52. Women make a lot of fuss about their need for independence, but also demand to be spoiled. Ironically, they do not see the conflict either.
53. People are getting more insecure due to our crooked social structure and values and thus they have become needier for attention and love. When they do not get it at the desired level, they feel even more lost and frustrated.
54. Relationships have become too important nowadays because people's basic needs are satisfied in modern societies rather easily. Without too many pressing issues and hardship to give them a real perspective of life, they fuss too much about love and happiness.
55. Relationships appear like the best antidote for loneliness, too, because we cannot live independently anymore despite all our pretensions.
56. However, providing constant attention to our insecure partners is also a major responsibility that causes anxiety besides all the extra work.
57. Relationships also force lifestyle changes and adaptation, often for fitting with our partners' (and their family's) habits and conflicting preferences.
58. Couples' insecurity and need for retaliation have reached such extremes that they kidnap, terrorize, or harm their own children just for intimidating their estranged partners.

The intensity of child custody battles also shows how inef-
fective our relationship mechanisms are.

59. All the above points demonstrate the huge challenge we,
especially the new generations, must face in order to find
better ways of relating instead of retaliating in their relationships.

60. For facing all these new challenges, it is necessary to view
gender differences in a more productive perspective, instead of being cynical and critical too much about them.
We must view them as a potent inner force that could help
genders complement each other and increase efficiency in
their relationships

The above facts reflect our legitimate concerns about the way
our deteriorating social setting is widening gender differences
and conflicts. Couples feel the rising turmoil and try to deal
with them somehow, but mostly blame their partners for their
relationship conundrums. Their feelings and complaints are
natural and understandable, but futile. We hurt one another in
relationships because of our stubbornness to see the bigger
picture and realize that relationship conflicts are, nowadays,
the symptoms of partners' idealism and progressive mentalities. We are merely criticizing one another for who we are
and insist on changing one another to our liking. We do not
wish to accept that people have the right to be and live as
they wish, especially since their odd attitudes, feelings, and
actions are driven by some deep personality attributes that
they cannot readily change. The problem is that our varied
qualities and quirks clash, especially in family relationships
where partners are too close physically and mentally and wish
to relate properly. The problem is that everybody ignores, or

actually often loves, his/her own idiosyncrasies, but resent other people's.

The symptoms of personality attributes often turn into major personal quirks that shake the foundation of relationships. These quirks are either real or merely the product of our perceptions due to our hasty, biased, and selfish judgments. Therefore, another task for every spouse is to stay patient and think a bit less selfishly to establish whether his/her partner's quirks are real or only his/her own perceptions due to unrealistic expectations from his/her partner or relationships in general. Neither our relationships, nor our partners, can be flawless, let alone perfect, never mind in the new era with all the complexities we have imposed upon relationships. Only learning about gender quirks and raising our sensitivity about them can somewhat alleviate the pressure on relationships.

Nevertheless, our harsh reactions to the sad reality of relationships in the new era would not solve anything. Instead, we must adjust our mentality a bit to envision the potential benefits of gender differences and make some use of them to increase synergy in relationships. In fact, personal attributes and quirks, like Ego, are often personal qualities that everybody needs for managing his/her life the best s/he can according to his/her limited intelligence in such a corrupt society. For example, both women's decisiveness and men's passivity are valuable attributes for them if they are exploited properly.

Of course, each gender must also recognize the symptoms of their unique personality attributes and the way they cause frictions in relationships. They must realize the impressions that their quirks, e.g., bossiness or procrastination make on their partners and cause deep conflict. Partners must admit that many of their seemingly logical habits may be symptoms of their personality flaws and quirks that can damage their relationships if they ignore them, or merely consider them natural, personal choices for living. As soon as we decide to be in a relationship, we lose a great deal of our natural rights and freedom for doing things as we like. Instead, a lot of diplomacy, tactfulness, and teamwork is required just to curb the irritating symptoms of our own natural personality attributes and tolerate the symptoms of our partners' natural personality attributes. A great deal of give and take is necessary to balance the symptoms of gender differences and other causes of relationship conundrums.

In particular, we must be acquainted with the prevalent gender quirks and qualities that infect relationships. We must anticipate and prepare for all the expected havoc in advance. Then we can test our patience for dealing with those rather idiotic, but common, symptoms in relationships before getting married. Couples should understand and sympathize with their spouses' idiosyncrasies and remember how some symptoms, e.g., decisiveness or procrastination, could lead to all sorts of misperceptions and misunderstanding in relationships without partners' intentions to hurt each other. Many examples of these conditions are discussed in this chapter and other parts of this book too.

Overall, the main purpose of discussing gender qualities and their symptoms, which ultimately lead to some seeming quirks, is to raise couples' awareness, patience, and sympathy for handling their relationship conundrums. If both sides (genders) see these fine points a bit more compassionately and show more flexibility and patience, the level of stress and conflicts would subside dramatically in relationships.

The next two chapters will discuss some of the genders' real and perceived quirks.

CHAPTER FIVE
Womanly Quirks

GENDER qualities and symptoms discussed in Chapters Three and Four emerge as personal quirks, especially when couples build their relationships and interact on a regular basis for fulfilling family responsibilities. Therefore, more details about these symptoms and quirks are presented in this and the following chapter.

It must be emphasized again, however, that the personal quirks discussed in this book are merely some common tendencies that erupt variably in both genders from time to time. However, we can attribute these symptoms and quirks to one gender more readily. Many exceptions exist for the type of quirks attributed to either gender, too, of course. For example, in some relationships, husbands are more decisive and bossy than their wives. However, the decisiveness and bossiness tendencies can be detected more often amongst wives. The prevalence and changes in these tendencies have a lot to do with culture and environment too.

In all, the main point is that, in almost all relationships, one spouse has a higher tendency in the twenty quirks that are noted in the following pages as either manly or womanly. As long as a difference in the level of some or all tendencies is

noticeable, the perceived and real quirks affect that relationship. Due to the low level of teamwork in relationships, almost
all relationships suffer from spouses' tendencies in the twenty
symptoms noted for men and women. Usually, one spouse is
bossier, one spouse is needier, one spouse is grouchier, one
spouse is more sensitive, etc. Yet the collection of quirks for
men and women are most typical in most relationships.

It must be also reiterated that the end purpose of all the
discussions about partners' quirks is only to raise couples'
awareness about the nature of the most prevalent obstacles in
relationships. Accordingly, the goal is to encourage more
teamwork, understanding, and sympathy between partners in a
relationship. The point is definitely not to criticize or condemn
the peculiar qualities of any gender.

Women's qualities and quirks are listed again below for
discussing each item in some detail.

Women's Qualities & Symptoms
Appearing as Quirks

1. Decisiveness ⟶	Bossiness/inflexibility
2. Activeness ⟶	Frustration/impatience
3. Neatness ⟶	Edginess/fussiness
4. Seeking Independence ⟶	Need more dependence
5. Optimism ⟶	Shortsightedness
6. Strong Identity ⟶	Resilience/bonding
7. Motherhood ⟶	Lesser role for men
8. Seeking Love ⟶	Romanticism/hopeful
9. High MLove ⟶	Release emotions
10. Seeking Adventure ⟶	Disgruntled

Decisiveness ⟶ Bossiness/inflexibility

Decisiveness is a high quality in our culture nowadays. However, our naïve intentions and motivations for decisiveness

cause mayhem in relationships instead of emerging as a quality. In fact, it is often imprudent to make a decision without a great deal of caution and our partner's cooperation. For one thing, the degree of accuracy of information required for every decision makes the matter of being a good decision maker quite difficult and risky these days. Therefore, just being decisive means trouble if a person erroneously assumes that s/he has all the necessary data for making a decision. Second, usually our intuition and emotions mislead us in using the proper decision criteria and making the right choices. Third, our tone of voice when expressing our decisions, and the arrogance that might radiate from it, can ruin the effect of any decision even if it were a useful one. Fourth, we should always leave a great deal of room for being wrong about our assumptions and decisions. The worst enemy of decisiveness is our dogmatism and a general tendency to be certain about our analysis, decision criteria, and conclusions.

The *Doubts and Decisions for Living* trilogy explains the perils of not only decision-making, but also people's certitude about their ideas. (See the list of the author's books at the beginning of the book.) Certitude that drives most of our decisiveness attempts is merely a sign of naiveté, stubbornness, and arrogance, and not a personal quality. In all, without maintaining some level of doubts about our viewpoints, our decisiveness is more a source of problem for ourselves and others than a life quality. Then when it turns into a habit of bossiness and inflexibility, the silliness of the situation and the damage it inflicts on our relationships become obvious.

Naturally, the practical purpose of our doubts is for keeping our guard in society, to avoid making hasty decisions and getting hurt. However, as a more important and personal purpose, maintaining some degree of doubts helps us keep our

sanity and humanness, because certitude only makes us too
dogmatic, arrogant, and stubborn. Without our 'doubts,' we do
not get the opportunity for self-awareness. Without our
'doubts' we forget how insignificant we humans are in the
large scheme of Creation and the universe. Without our
'doubts,' we would be even less instinctual and natural. And
without some doubts about the existing social structure and
values, we would never look for an alternative lifestyle, in
which our thoughts and behaviours are not manipulated, our
Egos and sense of superiority are not boosted senselessly, and
our lives are not so shallow and aimless.

Anyhow, women's decisiveness mostly reflects their reliance on their intuition (which imposes a definite point of
view), but also the influence of their strong Model telling them
that being indecisive is unattractive. However, decisiveness
makes women less patient and more stubborn with their positions or opinions. Then they are also sensitive and become
defensive when their decisions and viewpoints are not understood or acted upon immediately.

Active → Frustration/impatience

All the items on the list of women's qualities play a major role
in making women quite active, sometimes to the verge of obsessions. They are too active for keeping the household in
shipshape, neat and organized. They are active to implement
the barrage of decisions they make all the time and to make
sure the expected results are achieved. They are active to
prove and maintain their independence, to boost their identity,
to perform their maternal role most diligently, to find love, etc.
And if all these activities are not enough, they are quite adventurous and choosy that create a lot more concern and activity

for them. Their 'optimism,' as another quality on the list, makes them hopeful that they can achieve all these goals and perform all these activities. Accordingly, they are bound to face as many obstacles related to the large number of goals and activities they are thinking about and following at any point. Therefore, they often get frustrated and impatient when things do not happen as quickly or orderly as they wish.

Despite their drive for so many activities, women are not as much proactive in the sense of planning rather long-term and strategically. They are less proactive than they are pro activity. Even then, the type of activities they are so eager about, especially order and cleanliness, is the least valued by men. All their activities often appear like a big, noisy hoopla that cause more nuisance than add equivalent rewards. As men often perceive all these extra activities as quirks, women get more testy and frustrated for being criticized instead of appreciated for all these *special* efforts.

Neat and organized → Edginess/fussiness

For most women, there is no limit for neatness, order, and organization. The only problem is that not enough time is in a day to get everything they imagine necessary done!

I just cannot stop myself from quoting a real story that happened to me a few years ago during my first visit with a woman whom I had known from a distance but never had a chance to live with. When I visited her in her city of residence far away from mine, she asked me to wipe the water off the tiles surrounding the bathtub after every shower, the same way she did it herself. Between the two of us, we cleaned those tiles 2-4 times every day. She just could not bear the sight of the wet tiles, I guess. Her fussiness was directed not merely at the poor tiles, but also other stuff that did not involve my direct participation in cleanliness, especially that early in the morning.

I really liked her, though. She was highly educated, kind, beautiful, and had a great career. Therefore, when I returned to Vancouver after three weeks, I was quite eager to call her and ask her to marry me even though I was the one who had to move to a new city, so that she could keep her job. A writer can do his work anywhere, presumably. 'Fine,' I told myself, 'she is worth all my efforts.' However, I realized that I really could not clean the tiles after every shower for the rest of my life. I considered explaining my dilemma or confront her about the matter too. However, it was clear that she would either get really mad at me for refusing to do a simple thing she was asking me to do or resent me for having to do it herself after my showers, because she was adamant about the water-free tiles.

This episode surely reflects one of the extreme cases. Yet, this high quality in most women for order and cleanliness is just precious, except for causing unsettling dilemmas like the one I faced in the above story. In most relationships, some level of pressure is placed on both partners due to the women's need for order and cleanliness. At the other extreme, when a woman has no obsession with order and cleanliness, usually (but not always) the outcome is a complete catastrophe in terms of disorder and carelessness, even about the basic sense of hygiene.

Seek independence ➜ Need dependence

The most evident result of the new social setting and women's progressive role in professional life is the mix-up of our needs

for both independence and dependence personally and in relationships. We all need both our independence and dependence, but creating a right balance has become quite complex in
the new social setting. This matter is explained in detail in
Chapter Eight. It might help to read that section now, if you
wish. Here, the only point to emphasize is that women's new
social role goads them to look for more independence to affirm their identity, while deep down need more dependence
and support due to their emotional and MLove tendencies. At
the same time, the effect of all the changes in women's life in
the new era might gradually diminish their emotional tendencies and need for dependence that has been customary so far.
The outcome of all the qualities and symptoms listed for
women at the beginning of this chapter, especially their strong
identity, resilience, bonding, decisiveness, and many other
qualities and symptoms, has already changed some women's
mentality, including a lesser need for dependence. A large
group is nowadays emerging in political and corporate careers
with exceptional capacity to outdo men in all social roles due
to the combination of all the above noted qualities and symptoms. They can pursue and achieve such high objectives only
due to their ability to control their need for dependence on
others in order to focus better on their careers and ambitions.
A larger percentage of women might gradually build the same
level of tenacity for self-actualization and success in the future. However, at this point, the majority still has a high need
for dependence, while finding it in relationships has become
difficult and frustrating for them. The reason is that men and
women cannot balance their needs for both dependence and
independence either personally or in their relationships.

Optimistic ➤ *Shortsightedness*

Optimism makes women less conscious and concerned about the sources of conflicts in relationships, including the one noted above about the difficulty of creating a balance between our independence and dependence needs personally or in our relationships. Shortsightedness is a by-product of optimism, which hinders people's ability to see and accept the flaws with their present mentality about relationships. Instead, they strive to achieve their goals, including happiness and love, according to some unrealistic assumptions and criteria. These social and mental obstacles are explained in Chapters Seven and Eight.

Strong identity ➤ *Resilience/bonding*

No doubt, women have built a strong identity for themselves, at least in their minds and presentations. We see specific tactics and ideologies that they spread in their interactions. They have built an even deeper resilience due to their ability to bond and share their plans, success stories, and hurts. In line with the above discussions about women's eagerness for high independence, the stronger their identity becomes the more it might alienate them from men. This mayhem would heighten every year if a new mechanism for gender interactions and marital relationships are not developed and accepted by most of us.

Maternal ➤ *Lesser role for men*

As if women's emerging strong identity were not alienating men enough already, women's instincts, when added to life pressures and priorities, make them somewhat casual about men's needs. Instead, they focus on their children during the limited time they have in their busy daily lives. The symptoms of women's decisiveness and need for organizing the family affair quickly and effectively further make the matter of men's participation in family choices and routines more restricted. Therefore, men feel less included in the family decisions and not receiving enough respect in the family.

Seek love → Romanticism/hopeful

Despite all the above points about women's drive for identity and independence, and despite the emerging perception about their insensitivity toward men's needs, deep down they are not only quite sensitive, but also oversensitive quite often. Optimism mixed with the effects of the prevalent romantic impressions in the new culture and movies has made women hopeful about conquering love and tasting romance, while they like to enjoy their sexual freedom too. The inner conflict they have caused for themselves due to the low likelihood of reconciling their needs for both love and sex in the same relationship (or several relationships) over a long time is another source of mayhem in marital relationships.

Women are noted to be 'emotional.' The reasons are that they are vastly driven by their instincts and they have better control of Model. They can charm or even shed tears naturally to influence others. On the other hand, men are less capable of being charming or manipulative due to their supposedly logical minds and higher arrogance. Dependence on Model and intuition obviously makes women more emotional and vulnerable. Therefore, they have been forced to develop some type of defence mechanism to compensate for the side effects of their emotionality—by becoming a bit more practical than they are by nature. To do so, they have become more suspicious, calculating, and clever. This necessity has made them alert and eager to devise preventative measures for protecting themselves. This is another reason for them to become assertive. Then when they push the limits, of course, this assertiveness might lead to aggressiveness because the art of being assertive is not easy to master.

Women's sensitivity, on the other hand, leads to their higher expectations from relationships. They expect their spouses to understand their needs better, respond to their expectations more readily, etc. Since men are not equipped to understand and respond properly to this oversensitivity, more clashes and retaliations are introduced in relationships. Actually men cannot understand why women are so sensitive and react to simplest inconveniences so seriously. Women come across as too demanding nowadays because of their raw oversensitivity.

High MLove → Release emotions

On the one hand, women's ability to release their emotions helps them cope with the overall commotion and disappointments in society. Their attempts to at least share their hurts with one another help them immensely. On the other hand, the low social capacity (including men) to respond to women's natural sentiments feels frustrating and it becomes a cause for friction in relationships.

Women are more emotional partially due to their higher levels of the three love components, i.e., ELove, MLove, and SLove, again due to their instinctual urges. However, they are emotional also because they know better how to use MLove to express love better than men can. Men have little or no MLove aptitude, but they are equally suffering from the deprivations caused by their unfulfilled ELove and SLove. Men's natural resistance (due to their logical tendency) toward MLove often frustrates them too. However, not as much as it frustrates women, who do not understand why their MLove is unanswered, and why men are so incapable of MLove—romance.

Adventurous/choosy → *Disgruntled*

Women's craving for love and happiness naturally makes them more adventurous and choosy in order to make the best of life options and their time. Accordingly, they have grown high standards and expectations from life and relationships. Yet, again, life's realities hardly respond to all those dreams. Thus, women feel disgruntled, which in turn goads them to become more anxious and adventurous. This vicious cycle causes deep inner conflicts and turmoil for them. The outcome is that women take twice as much antidepressant to keep going in society and coping. Naturally, the effect of their optimism and misperceptions about life infect the health of their relationships too.

The overall effect of all these qualities and symptoms is apparent in the strong, peculiar *identity* that women portray in society nowadays and we can notice and feel it in all aspects of life. It is plausible that our value systems, including social mannerism and culture, are mostly a reflection of what women like. The reason is that women are the ones who support the ideas and customs within their households, but also across the society and nations by propagating them among themselves. They are more choosy about all values and norms. They are active, powerful around the family, decisive, manipulative, organizer, adventurous, intuitive, with a great deal of charm, maternal instincts, MLove, and a strong identity that they keep pushing its boundaries. What stronger force could there be for shaping the customs and desires of the population.

By the way, women's approach and desires fit extremely nicely with the goals of capitalism. Therefore, they get support from all the men and forces pushing capitalism to the extreme.

Studying the passive, submissive qualities of men in the next chapter supports the possibility of women's influence on shaping the characteristics of new societies even further. This might be a positive thing for redirecting the destiny of humanity and saving the planet from too much egoism, destruction, and greed that society has inflicted upon itself so far with its religions, wars, political and economic systems under men's rule. On the other hand, if women's success makes them equally egotistical and uncompassionate, then the future of human culture becomes even more questionable and doubtful, especially if all these changes keep alienating men and women while weakening the foundation of families too.

CHAPTER SIX
Manly Quirks

MEN'S ten qualities and related symptoms are precious in their own ways, but contradict women's almost line-by-line. Therefore, their role in causing couples' personal inner conflicts and relationship clashes are rather obvious. However, couples are not familiar with these basic facts about gender qualities and symptoms.

Men's Qualities & Symptoms
Appearing as Quirks

1. Cautious	Doubtful/indecisive
2. Passive	Submissiveness/laziness
3. Loose/Natural	Sloppy/disorganized
4. Seeking dependence	Need more independence
5. Realistic in general	Content
6. Poor Identity	Confused/depressed
7. Creative	Seclusion
8. Low trust in love	Unable to relate
9. Low MLove	Pent-up emotions
10. Preoccupied	Unresponsive

These qualities and symptoms are reviewed briefly in this chapter.

Cautious → *Doubtful/indecisive*

Obviously, everybody tries to use logic and patience to make better decisions instead of solely depending on intuition and allowing haste to take the best of them. However, men do it a little bit more than it seems necessary to women. It is plausible that men have always faced a wider range of external forces and threats than women have. Thus, they have gained a higher 'logic orientation' than women too. Conversely, women might have remained in closer contact with their instincts due to their maternal urges. However, intuition does not always provide the best answers for the problems of our modern societies. Instincts were good tools for primitive humans. Many of those instincts are still good guides for us in some instances. However, many of our instinctual urges are no longer effective for dealing with all sorts of artificial parameters and values that are introduced into our daily lives. Nowadays, instincts alone cannot respond to complex situations in society. And our logic, which men like to depend on a lot, is often contaminated by Ego anyway.

We can escape neither our doubts nor our need for making decisions. Planning our lives is an intuitive urge for intelligent people, yet our success depends on how well we analyse our options, doubts, and decision factors in a timely manner. Making the right choices in life is a complex task, especially since we suspect the reliability of information, social structure, and human nature. On the one hand, being proactive is becoming more important every day, considering our dynamic—and confusing—socioeconomic environment and the rising contamination of information base. On the other hand, we must understand the nature and importance of our doubts for managing our decisions objectively and patiently, while also making sure our doubts do not cause more mental stagnation.

This type of mentality about the difficulty of life choices is more prevalent among men—as historical breadwinners—and thus they are more cautious. Especially their apprehension feels too drastic compared with women who depend on their intuition, optimism, and a sense of adventure to take life in their strides more readily. More women are willing to live in the now than worrying about the repercussions of bad decisions. Men are usually more doubtful about their actions and decisions because they are more risk averse and depend on their raw logic for decision-making. This is true even though they have higher Ego and an urge to come across as decisive. Logic always requires an assessment of alternatives, which causes delays and uncertainty.

The reason women complain more often is because they like to make family decisions quickly and have no patience for men to fuss around every seemingly necessary project or be lazy with their decisions (due to their contemplation habits), especially when women feel something should get done right away.

Passive → Submissiveness/laziness

Men are rather passive due to their life outlook and realistic impressions of social values and interactions. However, they appear even more passive and lazy to women, which would then lead to family frictions. Two of the important points about gender qualities and quirks (as stated on page 14) are reiterated here about men's passivity:

1. Each gender quality and its symptoms are related to the other personality attributes (qualities and quirks) for that gender. For example, men's passivity is the outcome of their cautious mind, loose nature, realism, poor identity, etc. Thus, people cannot change their personality attributes readily even if they agreed they were destructive for them or their relationships.

2. Although genders' high qualities and symptoms irritate the opposite gender, without such disparity they would have tortured each other and ruined their relationships even more. Just imagine both genders being equally decisive and active based on their intuitions, or were both passive. Not only more frictions would have erupted all the time between partners, but also their whole life outcome would have become even more risky without at least some basic checks and balances that the present gender differences impose on relationships.

Therefore, men's passivity should be considered a blessing in some respects, too, while the irritation and frictions resulting form it cannot be lightly ignored either. Besides, men are most likely not passive by choice. Rather, their passivity could be due to forces of nature and society, for the purpose of coping and staying flexible, in hopes of fulfilling their need for dependence on a woman to some extent.

Loose/Natural → Sloppy/disorganized

Men are driven and preoccupied merely by their immediate needs, with less fanaticism, optimism, and adaptation aptitude. Thus, they have become relatively looser and more natural than women are. Women value social fad and etiquette and get influenced by commercials and new ideas faster. Therefore, men appear rather crude, sloppy, and disorganized to women. Thus, the question is which approach reflects and serves human nature and society better. Is it wise to get more phony and influenced by consumerism and showy lifestyles or try to keep as much of our naturalness as possible, although it makes men look sloppy and disorganized? Is life worth getting too hung-up about so many artificial needs and ambitions? Must we really keep propagating our superficial lifestyles as a symbol of progress and modernism?

Seek dependence → Need more independence

It sounds illogical to say that someone seeks dependence when he actually needs independence. Therefore, it must be clarified that everybody nowadays needs both dependence and independence, in some rotating priority. We have lower needs like food and shelter that we must satisfy first before directing our efforts toward satisfying higher needs like status or love. We all like to fulfil our higher needs because they give us a better sense of tranquility and self-worth. For men, in particular, the need for dependence is a lower need and independence is a higher need. Therefore, in order to strive and fulfil their need for independence, men must first take care of their need for dependence, which partially comes from companionship. Yet, for them, satisfying their basic dependence need is getting more complex and difficult because they cannot keep a companion without making so many sacrifices and concessions against their true nature and at the cost of losing more of their precious independence.

For women, the order is typically reversed because they value love and compassion that comes from dependence and companionship and because they need support to fulfil their highly potent maternal need and to raise their offspring. In fact, women's need for independence has mostly emerged in recent decades as they began seeking independence merely to establish a new identity for them.

In a sense, we can say that women's need for independence and men's need for dependence are newly developed needs, which are rather superficial like many other needs that the new social structure has planted in people's minds as new priorities.

Realistic → Content

Overall, men seem more realistic about life and its meaning than women are. Women are much more eager to define the meaning of life to enjoy every moment of their lives the best they can. However, men seem to have settled somehow better about the fact that life has no specific meaning; thus putting expectations on it would be a waste of energy on useless adventures that only cause frustration. They are content with a simpler lifestyle, although they keep working hard and follow their ambitions mostly to feel successful and have a better chance of finding the right kind of women for them.

Poor identity → Confused/depressed

As much as they try to impress women and keep them happy without losing their own integrity and self-image too much, men have only faced more resistance and rejection because their qualities and mentalities no longer match those of women's or the ones that women seek in a man. The outcome is obvious. Men have no *manhood or family* identity while pressured by women's strong (but crude) identity that keeps expanding without any target for bringing men and women together mentally.

Therefore, for the time being, men's confusion and frustration from the existing undefined means of gender communication would continue to hurt both their wives and their relationships.

Creative → Seclusion

The more men seek dependence and feel more deprived of it, the more mental seclusion they face. Women's maternal quality and attachment to their children make the matter worse when men find lesser importance in family while women focus on children. Women's sense of high achievement in creation of their children fulfils their high-level personal needs to a great extent, but also pushes men into mental and physical seclusion. Thus, some smarter men use the occasion to be creative in their own ways, although they might feel they cannot compete with women in that regard either. Nevertheless, they try to do their best to seek creativity for amusing themselves. Maybe they could impress women with their creativity too! The less creative men try to find other means of filling this gap in their lives.

Low trust in love → Unable to relate

Men's inability to relate is not totally their fault when we assess the way all the circumstances and symptoms of men's and women's personality traits (qualities) interact and make both genders rather sceptical about relationships, meaning of love, partners' sincerity, and all other gender's qualities. They have just become this way—so untrusting—and feel odd about the whole matter too. The only problem is that nobody seems to be looking for real solutions and to redefine relationships more in line with the new personal and social mentalities.

Low MLove → Pent-up emotions

Due to their higher passivity and looseness (living more naturally) in general, men's Model is less developed. Thus, they appear rather crude compared to women who have adopted social norms more heartily and adapted themselves rather perfectly. Men supposedly get together and bond, too, but their efforts are not deep and reliable in the way women are so good on this matter as well.

Accordingly, men usually have no or very little MLove to begin with due to their lower potentiality for Model or even perceiving (validating) love. Therefore, they know less about stirring up, or responding to, romance. Then they suffer more also at the time of separation because of their lower adaptability to change and relationship failure, again due to their lower Model and higher Ego. Lower capacity for Mlove also make men less capable of creating a balance between their ELove and SLove needs (or using their MLove to make up for the lack of ELove and SLove).

Preoccupied → Unresponsive

With all the symptoms and effects of men's qualities noted in this chapter, it is easy to see why men have been (appear) so preoccupied and unresponsive to women's demand for more romance and compliance. The only question is whether the matter will keep getting worse and out of hand eventually, or men can change to the liking of women. On the other hand, maybe both genders come to their senses and realize that only through teamwork and new mentalities they can minimize the level of frictions in relationships.

We cannot stop wondering about the effect of the emerging gender differences on the direction of human life. Are these new gender differences partly biological or mostly conditional due to our modern thinking. How are they going to change us and our relationships in the future? These topics are beyond the scope of this book, unfortunately. However, it seems reasonable, for example, to expect MLove increasing in men in the future after several decades of proper exposure to environments that might boost such a need in an authentic manner. They must build up some minimal trust gradually instead of being forced to play certain roles without deep conviction. Whether the situation in relationships would improve enough to bolster trust between men and women is a big question though.

PART III

Gender Quarrels

CHAPTER SEVEN
Gender Encounters

NEW social trends set the foundation for gender encounters and quarrels. We are living in a new era satiated with many shallow needs and ideologies by people who are too obsessed with finding love and happiness, but have no patience and compassion themselves. While genetics plays a role in gender differences, many outer forces in society deeply affect couples' mentality and behaviour in their relationships too, which then widen gender differences rapidly and imprudently. In fact, the fast-rising couples' conflicts and quarrels could be mostly attributed to the effects of social disorder, because genetics could have not changed this fast only over a few decades.

Chapter Four explained some of the general social setting that influences genders' attitude and relationships in different ways. This chapter reviews the details of new social trends and their impact on widening gender differences. Understanding the debilitating effects of these trends, especially couples' idiotic expectations from their partners, highlight the doom future of relationships and the roles that each gender is playing in that regard. After all, couples' awareness might help them modify their mentalities somewhat to create better means of teamwork and relating.

Relationship Facts

Gender differences are widening and partners quarrel more
often in the new era due to fast changes in social setting. In
particular, the following relationship facts have affected couples and their abilities to relate:

1. Our economic systems, mainly consumerism, are forming
   our social values. People have gained a great appetite for
   objects and ideologies, hoping to buy more things and happiness by accumulating wealth.

2. Consequently, the basic needs of relationships are ignored
   in the mass of superficial values, misperceptions, and naive
   slogans. 'Life is too short' and 'you live only once' have
   become the main mottos for most of us, especially women.
   Therefore, people jump out of their relationships to find a
   better partner and thus enjoy their presumed short lives the
   best they can. Women are more active on this matter (asking for separation), too—around 70% of all cases.

3. The increase in personal needs (for objects and compassion) has directly resulted in the decline of both moral and
   morale in society, while couples have raised their expectations from relationships enormously too.

4. The impact of unrealistic expectations from relationships
   has been two folds: First, it has created an additional sense
   of deprivation and personal stress that infects relationships.
   Second, we have come to believe that relationships can satisfy many of our emotional and financial needs. Couples
   assume that their partners are psychologically capable of
   providing all the love they seek. They demand more attention and affection to soothe their personal hurts and the
   stress of living in our chaotic societies. Therefore, in effect,
   they are weakening the potency of their relationships.

5. Couples try to live beyond their means, at a higher standard of living than they can afford or deserve. This is an added source of pressure, while partners strive to find that elusive happiness at all cost. They demand more regardless of their means. Family debt per capita in relation to their income is at its highest level ever, due to crooked family values and consumerism. Family crises are getting out of hand due to the lack of partners' sensibility about budgeting and their finances.

6. New societies have advocated the concepts of equality and individualism relentlessly. Partners' drive for independence and identity has turned relationships into a battleground for establishing their territory and superiority. Thus, the role of teamwork in relationships is not gaining the needed attention.

7. We put our personal needs ahead of the relationship needs. We abandon our relationships more often by the simplest signs of inconvenience. We want to give ourselves the highest chance of finding happiness in another relationship as soon as possible.

8. The traditional principles that guided relationships in the past have been abolished and there are no new principles to direct couples anymore. No standards exist for couples to measure the health of their relationships by. Thus, they rely on their own subjective viewpoints or the advice of friends and family to justify their crooked conclusions about the state of their relationships.

9. Couples consider 'love' the main factor for relationship success, not only for starting one, but also for sustaining it. The problem with this approach has been discussed in Chapter Eight.

10. Relationships have become too complex and more demanding. Couples are unaware of the relationship needs, the psychological effects of their encounters, and how deeply they are affected by their genes and rearing conditions. Furthermore, they forget that people's mindsets or personalities cannot be changed simply because their partners are expecting them to change.

11. The number of divorces has skyrocketed in the last few decades. At this time, it has passed 50% mark and is approaching 60%.

12. The amount of frustration and stress in the surviving relationships is increasing, too, due to partners' oversensitivity and unfulfilled expectations from relationships. Partners are also burdened by their indecision about staying in or leaving their dysfunctional relationships.

13. Stress levels in society and organizations have risen drastically due to the complexity of work and interactions, employment uncertainties, discriminations, international competition, and the authorities' obsession to serve themselves instead of attending to their social responsibility.

14. The level of stress in families has also increased because, nowadays, usually both partners work outside the house and are exposed to extreme pressures, especially women, who have been subject to more abuse and discrimination in organizations.

15. All the bad values and habits of organizations, such as hypocrisy, power struggle, and arrogance have infected family relationships too. Partners follow the same rules to assert themselves at work and at home. Some women might actually perceive their husbands as abusive bosses in the work environment as well as at home.

16. Personal stress due to social demands and substandard relationships makes couples testy and impatient in their relationships. They bug each other exactly at the time that life is confusing enough and out of control already. And they expect each other to be more romantic too!

17. To remedy relationship problems and enhance communication, counsellors encourage role-playing and love expressions. Yet, relationship problems keep rising. This trend shows that the existing schemes, especially role-playing, are not working. Obviously, unless partners are naturally convinced about the feelings or words they exchange, their relationship would only worsen. All these role-playings, as well as phony values, have made couples lose their identity and authenticity.

18. Companionship is probably the most important (basic) need of individuals nowadays and the one that is most often left unfulfilled. The importance of 'need for a companion' is evident in the wide range of personal needs it could potentially cover. Most people think and dream about a good companion as much as they think about food, consciously or subconsciously—as a kind of need urgency.

19. A crucial fact that couples ignore when they start their relationships is that, **nowadays the chances of relationships failing are higher than surviving.** The idea of finding a soul mate usually turns into a sour fate when they only end up in substandard relationships. Couples ignore this vital fact at the outset and do not do enough soul-searching and planning in advance.

20. Couples are not trained and prepared to handle neither the relationship needs, nor the most likely scenario in their relationships, i.e., separation.

The Effects of Emerging Trends

The above fundamental facts and other discussions in this book paint the reality of relationships in the new era. In this section the effects of the emerging trends on relationships are reviewed. Gender differences are playing a major role in the havoc noted below and the emerging environment is itself creating more gender differences. These examples show the complexity of relationship conundrums. Yet, they barely scratch the depth of relationship problems. They reflect that reversing the deteriorating situation of relationships would be an uphill struggle and quite time-consuming. In particular, the basis for gender quarrels are analysed in some detail in this chapter. **All references like 'people', 'men', 'women' or 'we' do not mean everybody, but rather a significant portion of that particular category.**

21. People seem to be living in a fantasy world with substantial needs and dreams. Their ambitions and needs for objects do not necessarily match their talents and efforts, and their needs for affection do not match their capacity to exchange compassion. Even when they are given wealth and compassion, they abuse it because they are not mentally prepared to handle them responsibly. The more their selfish needs are satisfied, the more arrogant and greedier they become. Yet, everybody believes he/she deserves more love and things.

22. Accordingly, couples' rising superficial needs, including unrealistic expectations from relationships, have crippled the social structure to provide social services and maintain a healthy environment.

23. The increasing amount of unfulfilled expectations from relationships has also led to a great deal of frustration, retaliation, and hostility in families and society. Partners' oversensitivity due to untamed expectations has obscured even simple communications. For example, we hear often nowadays, especially from women, a phrase such as, "He/she does not know how to spoil me!" Many relationships break down every day because of this odd expectation. They do not even mind saying it so bluntly, as if 'spoiling' is a reasonable demand for relationships in the new era. Especially, after years of exploitation by men, now women want to be spoiled as if making up for the lost compassion of past generations. They seek ELove, attention, and sometimes obedience too.

24. The level of misperceptions and miscommunications in relationships have increased very fast, too, and created more havoc.

25. For one thing, couples have lost their sense of objectivity about the purposes and potentials of relationships, because they have become too idealistic and emotional about their expectations from relationships.

26. Accordingly, couples continue to jump out of their relationships faster and faster because they believe they can find another partner to fulfil their expectations better and give them the love they deserve. Most of us struggle all our lives in search of an ideal relationship. Only a few of us might eventually realize our naivety after repeated failures.

27. Both single and married people envy each other's position and lifestyle. Everybody wishes to have the advantages of both lifestyles.

28. Married people jump out of their relationships fast because of their misperceptions about a single (independent) life and the possibility of finding a more appropriate mate.

29. And unmarried people look for an ideal partner obsessively to complete their social identity, while they keep bragging about their freedom as a single person.

30. Besides our pleasure seeking mentality in the new era, our erratic urges for both dependence and independence are obviously playing a role in creating many misperceptions about relationships too.

31. We have turned into a special (spoiled) generation—asking for more love while becoming more arrogant at the same time. We do not realize that with more arrogance, we keep losing our capacity to give and receive love.

32. Our children are getting even more spoiled in terms of idealism and not appreciating the hardships of life. Therefore, the deteriorating trends in relationships would go downhill for some time to come.

33. Couples are unaware of the true success factors for relationships. So they continue to insist on love and objects as the main requirements.

34. Couples judge the health of their relationships arbitrarily or based on phony values, because there are no authentic yardsticks for setting practical standards and measuring the success of relationships.

35. Couples have little patience and interest to learn about the basic problems of relationships in a serious manner, e.g., reading books like this one. At best, people have only time and patience for learning about some possible quick fixes, which have no ultimate value anyway. People read those kinds of books or follow a few of counsellors' advices only

to show that they did something to improve their relationships and still it did not work.

36. The increasing rivalry and clashes between men and women look like some kind of all out gender warfare. The level of insults, belittling, retaliations, intimidations, abuse, manipulation, badmouthing, power struggles, competition, crying, making a scene, screaming, blackmailing, and trying to outsmart one another just keep increasing.

37. Men and women are becoming increasingly alienated due to the changing social values and couples' drive to establish their gender identities better (usually at the cost of weakening the other gender's identity). As noted in the previous chapters, some inherent gender differences are also adding fuel to the matter of couples' alienation in relationships.

38. Many of the clashes between men and women are due to women's higher instinctual tendency challenging men's higher logical predisposition.

39. In reality, however, both our instincts and logic are usually flawed anyway. Therefore, often, nobody is right due to their erroneous perceptions and lack of objectivity.

40. Then problems increase because men and women want to change each other's decision processes, i.e., to make them more logical or intuitive—more like themselves. They fail because the instinctual urges of women and the logical tendencies of men are too deep to change quickly even if they realized the need for it. Their inherent personality traits often hinder this change to happen.

41. All along, personal failures in relationships, ongoing clashes, and sad statistics keep increasing mistrust among partners. Yet, people still ask for more love to justify their relationships, define their lives, and find happiness. The big contrast is obvious when people in-

sist on love while the overall trust is fading fast in society. Love in the absence of trust! How could couples really be sincere about their love expressions when deep down, in their subconscious, their sense of mistrust about people, including their partners, linger?

42. It is hard to believe that 'trust' can be rebuilt between genders as a general social norm in the near future and couples become truly convinced about it.

43. Therefore, while couples pretend to start their relationships based on trust, deep down they remain justifiably sceptical about it. This is true despite their convincing expressions of love and the roles they play mostly through MLove.

44. Overall, it is naïve to depend on 'love' or 'trust' to build a relationship. Instead, couples need objective mechanisms and a relationship framework to map their joint life.

45. All those sleeping around with different partners and then talking about finding love are not congruent values or plans. Satisfying our sexual urge is a practical choice in modern society, but confusing it with love is hypocritical and impractical. The meanings of love, lust, and trust have become too intermingled and convoluted. This is causing additional mistrust and shakier social values.

46. The conflict caused by less trust and more demand for love is felt deeper by men. This is because men supposedly have higher logical tendencies than women who are more emotional according to the discussions in this book. With their lower MLove and Model, men are already handicapped in expressing love, but when trust is gone, the matter of expressing love becomes even more awkward for them. Women are more capable of expressing love, even when their trust is not high. This is due to their higher MLove and Model, of course. Men lack this flexibility but women

have a hard time accepting this fact and instead wonder why men are so passive most often.

47. The general level of trust in relationships, and trust about our partners' words, would keep declining in line with the upward trend in relationship failures. Thus, expressing love with honesty would become even more difficult, especially for men.

48. Accordingly, men usually give up the possibility of finding a soul mate sooner than women do. They continue to look for a companion nonetheless, but not with the aim of finding love. They seek a companion mostly out of loneliness and for satisfying their basic needs. Women continue to remain more romantic and optimistic about finding a soul mate due to their higher intuitiveness and Model.

49. In fact, women appear to have a higher need and talent for all three levels of love, i.e., ELove, MLove, and SLove than men. This aptitude pushes them to pursue love at any cost, but also get depressed for failing.

50. Couples are unaware of their personal flaws and also how badly everybody gets damaged psychologically during their relationship experiences. They believe that not only they are flawless, but also there are enough perfect people out there to choose for companionship. Therefore, they keep searching for some untenable ideal life that matches their fantasies.

51. In the older times, people used to believe that marriage's most important objective was for partners to share the hardships of life together. Couples knew how difficult life really is. They were ready and willing to make personal sacrifices and help each other sincerely. They played their angelic roles to reduce each other's burdens.

52. However, nowadays many couples do just the opposite. For one thing, people are pushing themselves to stay positive and believe that life is splendid and manageable. Therefore, instead of sharing life's hardships, they create more burdens for each other with a slight sign of inconvenience. Their unrealistic expectations and dreams about happiness make them view any nuisance an unacceptable barrier in their lives. And they want to abandon their partners rather quickly for the greener pastures. Today's marital objectives are mainly revolving around partners' fixation for love, sexuality, and happiness.

53. Women have a harder time in satisfying their conflicting needs for dependence and independence than men do. This is due to the emphasis nowadays for women to seek independence as a means of establishing their identity. This pressure aggravates their already conflicting (instinctual) urges for both dependence and independence.

54. Instinctually, women drive for security and dependence more than men do. In addition, the more independence they acquire, the more dependence they crave. This is because their exaggerated search for independence hinders the natural fulfilment of their need for dependence. For example, women are more eager to find love and a social partner, because they not only are more optimistic about the possibility of finding their soul mate, but also crave love harder instinctually—due to their higher need for adaptation (Model) and the urge for reproduction.

55. Therefore, on the one hand, women like to depend on men, for procreation and for fulfilling their higher social needs due to their higher Model. On the other hand, they feel the urgency to assert their identity by proving their independ-

ence and equality. This dilemma creates inner conflict and confusion for women and widens the gender gap.

56. Seeking more independence is also a matter of 'life phase' for women, while raising and enjoying their kids. They feel empowered and independent due to their maternal power, but also because they presume their men are sticking around for emergencies anyway. Once their kids are gone, however, their need for dependence takes precedence again, especially if men have strayed.

57. Inherently, women need dependence on men also for support and to complete their social identity, though they might not wish to show or accept this fact.

58. Men's conflict in terms of dependence/independence is straightforward and simple. They seek independence instinctually, but need to depend on women to fulfil some of their basic needs, including compassion and sex. They appear helpless without women, while inherently they continue to value their own independence highly.

59. Nonetheless, both genders strive for both dependence and independence regularly, though for completely different reasons. They go through these cycles even more forcefully at some stages of their relationships. They start a relationship to fulfil their need for dependence (mostly their basic needs, e.g., sex and ELove). Soon, however, they take their relationship for granted and press for a complex need like independence (according to their naïve perceptions of independence.)

60. There is a race in society to behave pompously, strive for a lot of things and compassion, and be highly competitive. Everybody also likes to be highly sociable, pretentious, and popular. When people go to work on Mondays, they keep

asking one another what they did on the weekend as if gauging a person's worth and completeness.

61. Humans' inner conflicts are responsible for their confusion, stress, and suffering in life, which eventually affect their relationships too. Overall, humans' *elementary* inner forces to be good are always in conflict with the external forces goading them to be bad. The modern society advocates greed, hypocrisy, dominance, and arrogance just to name a few of the crooked trends in the new era.

62. People have become too calculating and opportunistic (users), due to their negative experiences and conditioning, including their conviction that life is too short and precious. They use various schemes to strengthen their positions and get ahead, and they associate with people whom they find useful to them in some ways. This general perception (about people's hypocrisy, calculating nature, and insincerity) affects relationships, too, because partners judge each other based on their shallow criteria of life, but also their overall mistrust.

63. How can people be romantic when most of them are only trying to be practical (by being so calculating and materialistic) in such a chaotic environment? These are contradictory objectives. Our social setting is ruining people's perceptions of one another and 'love'.

64. Couples are becoming less capable nowadays to perceive and judge their relationships in its totality. They are easily influenced by their own need urgencies, and they are easily irritated by single events. The overall advantages of relationships are largely ignored due to hasty egotistical judgments based on emotional episodes and erroneous perceptions.

65. There is a 'typical woman' image developing in the new era mostly due to women's recent efforts to achieve equality, individualism, and independence. They have created and portrayed a special role and identity for themselves. On the other hand, men have not yet tried to create and propagate an identity for themselves. They have not been active in projecting a picture of a typical man.

66. Yet men are stereotyped as selfish and unromantic. In reality, however, men are simply lost and without identity, nowadays, because they have difficulty understanding and coping with women's new demands. They have difficulty defining and asserting themselves at this time.

67. Women have been able to bond and support one another to set the rules of relationships. They are creating a new culture that might eventually prove quite dysfunctional for maintaining relationships.

68. An advantage of women's bonding is that they get plenty of support when they leave their relationships. On the other hand, because of this bonding, and in line with the women's general attempt to propagate the new culture, they encourage each other to be least tolerant of their relationship flaws and abandon their spouses quickly.

69. Therefore, while women seem to help each other in terms of support after separation, they might also be screwing up each other and causing more separations, *maybe even intentionally,* by provoking one another with their progressive ideas and attitude.

70. Men, on the other hand, do not have a sense of empathy, nor enough Model, to soothe each other's hurts once they leave their wives. Part of this deficiency is because men keep their emotions private to protect their pride. Women show their emotions but move on faster.

71. Women are emotionally stronger by nature, and also due to their higher social adaptability and Model. This helps them in terms of rebounding quickly after separation. And then the support they receive from other women helps them recover even faster and better. However, the same need for social adaptability and Model makes them quite anxious to find a new companion.

72. Women's intuitiveness, higher Model, and bonding ability also give them more resilience and optimism about life and love, which help them adapt better to changes and disappointments. Overall, they do not get too discouraged by their failures in past relationships. Yet the number of women on anti-depressants is twice that of men.

73. Conversely, it usually takes longer for men to heal their wounds and recommit themselves to another relationship, due to their lesser resilience and the lack of support after separation. This additional agony teaches them better lessons. Therefore, they usually delay getting into serious relationships.

74. Men's logic and mistrust usually override their emotional needs, unlike women. Yet their lower social adaptability makes them more vulnerable in terms of submitting to women's whims out of loneliness—but not necessarily out of love.

75. Due to their pessimism about finding a soul mate, men are becoming passive and this is making women frustrated, and more assertive.

76. Women are more social instinctually. They seek a companion to fit and feel better in social gatherings, to complete their identity, and for support. Therefore, they do not seek men necessarily out of love, loneliness, or merely for the sake of having a companion. They already have many

companions in other women. Satisfying their social and security needs often takes precedence even over their craving
for love.

77. Conversely, men prefer some seclusion and privacy. Thus,
their need for a companion is more for avoiding total loneliness. Men like socializing too, of course, but it is not their
main motivation for finding a companion. Besides their
primitive urge to create variety in their lives, men's socializing motives are mainly for complying with family values
and making their wives happy, to be perceived as a sociable person.

78. Despite the women's urge for a companion, and their obsession to enjoy life at its fullest, the welfare of their children often gets a higher priority. Many women postpone
their serious relationships with another man, after a marriage breakdown, until they feel their children's relative independence or readiness. Therefore, considering the sacrifice most women make for their children, they believe they
deserve their children's higher love, which they usually receive more than fathers do.

79. Fathers' traditional respect has diminished in families for
several reasons. **First,** women have assumed the ultimate
role and responsibility for raising children and they perform this difficult task with absolute authority and decisiveness. Children find their mothers in charge and their fathers passive with much less authority around the family.
Second, mothers really dedicate themselves to their kids,
who in turn take a keen note of their mothers' devotion.
Children feel a higher bond with their mothers instinctually, too, the same way mothers feel toward their children.
Third, children see their mothers more vulnerable and
needy for attention, especially because women can show

their vulnerability through Model cleverly. Therefore, children feel obliged to take care of their mothers more than they see a need to sympathize with their fathers.

80. The bottom line is that men feel less involved with children and not receiving adequate love and respect. Their wives actually treat them a lot like another one of the children, including the use of an authoritative tone in their conversations with their husbands.

81. Nonetheless, the lower level of respect and power for fathers has made a negative impact on the health of the whole family.

82. The overall trend reiterated in this book shows that women have rather succeeded in creating and expressing their new strong identity after many decades of oppression by men. They have learned to be assertive and support one another to establish their individuality and identity. Conversely, men have lost theirs due to the ambiguity of the gender roles and new relationship expectations. This is an accurate picture overall, yet the final outcome is questionable. For one thing, women's success to enforce their identity depends a lot on men's reaction to their demands and the roles that women expect of them to play. More importantly, both men and women can truly attain, and feel comfortable with, their identities only if they have a companion. Our endless, inherent urge to find our soul mates is the best indication of our sense of incompleteness (lack of full identity) without a good companion. Our need for a companion is an urgent and important need. It can potentially satisfy a large number of personal needs of humans stretching from the basic need for sex to the spiritual need for SLove. When these needs are not satisfied, few humans might at-

tain enough psychological independency to affirm their identity in the new era.

83. Women may pretend that they understand, and are happy with, their emerging identity. However, when they reflect on their lives, they notice that their identity is incomplete and hurtful without a companion. Indeed, they need a man in their lives more than ever nowadays; more than men need a woman. This is due to women's higher Model and eagerness for social activity.

84. Therefore, women's identity is questionable without a man or while they are not happy with their companion. For one thing, they would be too preoccupied with the task of finding their soul mate, as they are optimistic about finding an ideal partner. As stated before, men are not so optimistic about finding a soul mate, and they are less obsessed about having a companion (or even an identity) due to their lower Model.

85. Therefore, if women's drive for identity reduces their chances of finding or keeping *competent* men in their lives, they would never find their true identity. No matter how much resilience and assertiveness they try to reflect in a presumably strong personality, deep down they feel a vacuum. 'Competent' refers to men who supposedly have a strong character (identity). No woman would enjoy or respect a man with a weak character. A man without a strong identity is worthless even for women. Yet, many women do not mind weakening their husbands' spirits.

86. Overall, it seems that many women prefer to intimidate and control their spouses than respect them. This mentality has been true for men, too, throughout the history of humanity and now women are feeling the need to the same thing, de-

spite their push for equality and mutual respect in modern societies.

87. Accordingly, it seems that both genders are getting more entangled with ongoing power struggles, because they find intimidating and manipulating their spouses the only option to manage their relationships.

88. It is absurd that all these conflicting forces are somehow corrupting relationship environments. Men are confused and lost for the time being anyway. However, their innate resistance and passivity are indeed damaging women's attempt to assert their own identity. This is especially true when the outcome is women's lesser access to *competent* men to support them mentally and physically.

89. Having emphasized on the fact that both genders need a companion to find their true identity, a more distressing fact must be stressed again as well. That is, even when they are in a relationship, neither gender can find their identities because of all their clashes.

90. Thus, genders' attempts to find their identities fail whether they are in a relationship or not, unless they adopt a more practical relationship framework to relate more effectively. The reason is that as long as the parameters for creating their identities are not pure and unselfish, partners continue to fight in order to enforce their perceptions of ideal identities for their genders.

91. In another word, partners' misperceptions of themselves and their partners, as well as their erroneous impression of ideal identities for their genders, prevent them from finding their true and practical identities. Besides, their continuous clashes suck the energy out of them to find and exert their true identity.

92. A cynical observation about relationships in the new era is that sometimes women seek men mostly to test and exert their power over them; to prove their superiority and new identity.

93. Two types of role-playing are introduced in relationships, both with adverse effects. First, the role-playing schemes that marriage counsellors advocate in order to stir up communication and love in relationships. The weakness of this technique is that as long as the real problems of a relationship are not understood by partners, playing roles only frustrates them further. All the superficial communications actually confuse them more and drive them away from the reality of their relationship. Instead, they must somehow grasp and tackle the main sources of their problems directly.

    The second type of role-playing has even a harsher impact on relationships. It begins from the minute partners meet and it continues throughout their relationship. They play all kinds of roles and games to impress, entice, manipulate, or deceive each other. They exaggerate in all respects in order to succeed: by flattering, getting too emotional, showing indifference, proving their independence and power, retaliating, and so many other games that go on throughout the process of dating and in their relationship too.

94. Couples like to play certain roles in order to set precedence and enforce their needs. They strive to set artificial boundaries to establish their superiority from the beginning. So, it is becoming impossible to sense sincerity and the true personality of people nowadays. This role-playing (including retaliations or reactions as defence mechanisms) might be somewhat justified considering that everybody gets hurt in

relationships at some point. They play games to prevent more headaches. But then, they lose the chance of relaxing and being natural, which could indeed improve their relationship significantly.

95. By playing games, couples have minimized their own level of objectivity as well as their partners'. Thus, they suffer personally while their relationships follow a destructive course too. By role-playing, couples are also losing the opportunity of finding companions who appreciate them for who they really are. Instead, they only struggle with their own phony personalities (to appear convincing and natural), as well as with their partners' (to understand them perhaps).

96. Nowadays, most people like to depend on their clever Model to play appealing roles for attracting love and sympathy. At the same time, they also try to hide their strong Ego and haughtiness behind Model. In a society where arrogance has found such a strong value, even Model often advocates pomposity. So, it is becoming difficult to understand who a person really is.

97. Women are becoming more active socially and placing a high value on living life to its fullest. They need to do more things, go to various functions, and travel extensively. At the same time, men are becoming more passive, content, and couch potatoes, partly due to the declining chances for maintaining good relationships.

98. It is fair to say that women are the stronger gender overall. Men are a weaker gender, in terms of emotional vulnerability (personality), despite the fact that women are more emotional. The reasons for this seeming contradiction are explained throughout this chapter. Actually, men's weakness is widely known and propagated regularly in the new

era. Even advertising agencies exploit this perception whenever they can benefit from it (see note 114 below). Women are also aware of men's vulnerability. Therefore, it is natural that they might attempt to use this information to push their ideologies and obtain everything they believe they deserve.

99. Due to their higher reliance on intuition, decisiveness, and the teachings of the new culture, women are trying to be in charge of the family. They seem to be good at it, too, in many respects. However, in the process, they also feel the need to prove their superiority to men. Well, since women are the stronger gender in reality, why should not they be in charge or try to show off their superiority occasionally? The problem is that any type of superiority by either gender cannot work in the new era where the emphasis must be placed on equity, individualism, independence, and satisfying personal needs.

100. Thus, when women try to prove their superiority, it leads to further deterioration of relationships and more mistrust. Except, of course, in the cases where husbands prefer to be completely passive and/or submissive. Many women actually do not mind turning their spouses into submissive men in order to feed their own Ego and ELove. Some women might think: "Why not give it a try anyway and see if it works." However, in the end, this situation cannot prevail in progressive relationships.

101. Relationships would go through a lengthy, unpredictable transition period while women try to assert themselves and find their identity.

102. During this transitional period, women have difficulty being a modest (content) wife in an environment which advocates a domineering attitude to enforce equality and

identity. Many women have been successful in practicing this approach in their relationships already. They present very appealing role models for the rest of them.

103. In fact, women's influence over one another is too strong to be ignored, by either women or men. Mothers, daughters, female colleagues and friends are all placing a lot of pressure on one another nowadays to behave assertively. Any woman who attempts to behave differently might be ousted. More importantly, however, she would feel miserable for not being a typical (assertive) woman like others.

104. It is quite likely that many men have become passive and submissive, because they have less capability for bonding together and are thus becoming weaker. Furthermore, they are less eager to develop and maintain a strong identity for themselves. Their logical minds, passivity, and neediness for a companion are keeping them the weaker gender they have probably always been psychologically and emotionally.

105. Men's resort to violence and physical domination are indeed good clues about their inability to keep up with the kind of games that women are better at playing so naturally. Men's frustration is also due to their inability to keep up with women's needs and demands, which men often find illogical often anyway.

106. Women seem to be winning most of the battles in relationships, but it is doubtful that any gender can win the war that is going on. The point is that, as long as one gender or one partner is weaker than the other, their relationship remains dysfunctional. There would not be enough respect and challenge for the stronger partner to stay in the relationship or take it serious enough. This fact is indeed most

relevant in our new culture where individualism and self-esteem have found such a high value.

107. Therefore, women's urge to establish their superiority in the new era would not benefit anybody in the long run. Women are behaving naturally, of course, according to their inherent personality strengths and strong bonding capability. Nonetheless, their effort is already putting relationships in great jeopardy. They would be (are) the ones suffering the most from the repercussions of the existing situation, because they are more sensitive and they believe in love.

108. Obviously, relationships get into trouble because both partners are at fault in some respects. And also because the whole society is losing control over both the economy and relationship norms. Even when a partner is smart, patient, and humble to make the relationship work, the prospects of saving his/her relationship might still be gloomy. The reason is that his/her modest behaviour is perceived as a sign of weakness instead of goodness. He/she is treated poorly or ignored. So both partners are normally forced to be assertive, which usually turns into aggressiveness and quarrels.

109. The situation with relationships resembles the global warming mayhem. Nobody is willing to accept the existence of a fundamental problem or do anything about it. The main reason, also like global warming, is the economy. Materialism and hypocrisy would not allow partners to become more realistic about the values surrounding them.

110. Women go into their next relationships with even more expectations instead of less. They believe that their reasons for leaving their past relationships (e.g., need for more love

or compassion) had been justified, and thus their new relationships must make up for everything they had missed before. They want to prove to themselves and others that they made a right decision to leave their previous relationships. Therefore, they look for more love, luxury, and security. Conversely, men usually prepare themselves for less authority and set lower expectations if they decide to get into another serious relationship.

111. An effect of women's intuitiveness is that their priorities somewhat change after having their children. For one thing, they are forced to exercise a lot of authority to make their children follow their rules. A mother is driven instinctually to manage her life as well as her children's. Therefore, she becomes authoritative, commanding, and demanding. These are mostly instinctual traits that surface when her life begins to get hectic with children, and maybe a lazy husband, testing her patience. She also finds less time for her husband after children are born. He is suddenly given a lower priority and importance, maybe not intentionally but rather practically. Furthermore, she learns eventually that it is more efficient and natural to treat her husband like another one of her children. Decisively, she has to get things organized and done quickly the way she has found productive through her child-rearing experiences. She finds these tactics, i.e., commanding, demanding, and impatience, most natural and effective for running the family affair.

112. For men, however, their wives' gradual (but drastic) change feels unnatural and annoying eventually. They attribute it to their wives' loss of interest and romance. In this environment, women look rather insensitive, impatient, and

sometimes even cruel, in the way they run the whole household, including their husbands.

113. Some partners, especially men, learn to stay passive in order to cope with their substandard relationship situation. Overall, women play a more active role in shaping the relationship atmosphere and imposing the rules due to their decisiveness. Men, on the other hand, are lazy to argue or fuss too much. Therefore, more women are becoming in charge of the family, while men are getting more submissive.

114. The existing culture does not give too much room for teamwork. Actually, an image of men's submissiveness (and maybe their idiocy) is propagated regularly even in TV commercials to sell products to women. For example, while writing the facts about gender differences, a couple of TV commercials caught the author's eyes. They reflect how social trends regarding relationships are grasped and exploited even by advertisers:

The first commercial was about Multigrain Cheerios. The box apparently refers to 120 calories per serving. The husband makes an innocent comment to his wife: "Are you trying to watch your diet?"

"Do I look like I need to watch my diet?" the wife asks with irritation and sarcasm.

"No, honey, I'm just stating what the box says (about its low calories)," the poor husband replies with a guilty tone in absolute panic.

"What clsc thc box says?" the wife demands.

"The box says, 'Shut up, Steve.'" the husband replies with shame and misery. The wife smirks.

The second commercial was about McCain's Deep and Delicious frozen cake. The wife is enjoying the cake. And the husband is trying to draw his wife's support about his dream of becoming a mime. However, she is not paying attention to his comments and enactment of some miming gestures, because she is absorbed by the taste of the cake. When she notices him finally, she demands with impatience, "What're you doing?"

The husband freezes in his miming gesture like a lamb suddenly facing a lion. "I'm living my dream," he replies with total panic and desperation again. "Stop it," the wife orders him.

The husband stops, scared stiff and mute. The commercial ends. The wife makes the ruling and that is the end of the story for the husband who likes to live his dream of becoming a mime.

Humour is supposedly the intention of these commercials, to sell their products. However, they are propagating men's passivity and subordination in relationships in the new era—which is largely true but not a proper viewpoint. They exploit the fact that men are put down by women and they cannot do a darn thing about it. They believe it is funny! They advocate women's power, all for the sake of flattering and encouraging them to buy their products.

115. These commercials reflect the reality of relationships, but also propagate arrogance. They find it funny that women's superiority is becoming part of our acceptable culture, including aggression toward men. How are we going to convince ourselves that these values are destructive for both men and women? How many years will we need to be convinced? Probably a century is a good guess!

116. If someone asks the author to identify the most destructive force damaging relationships and widening gender differences, he would suggest 'Hollywood.' Those naïve love

stories, senseless gender confrontations, and meaningless conclusions have been contaminating the brains of the public all over the world. Some ignorant writers are doing everybody a disservice by their unrealistic, simple-minded scripts. A scene in the movie *Two Weeks Notice* with Sandra Bullock and Hugh Grant is really confusing and interesting: Sometime in the middle of the night, Sandra is returning a pair of shoes that she had borrowed from her friend—a weird timing all by itself. After the friend goes down and opens the door, they sit down near the curb to talk. The friend's husband appears at the window of their apartment, looks down into the street with concern, and says, "Everything's okay?" The wife yells at him with unbelievable attitude, "Not now! Everything is not about you!" Her comment and tone of voice has no relevance and meaning in that scene or in the context of the whole movie. It only reflects the absurdity of relationships' atmosphere. "Okay," the husband mumbles with apprehension as he withdraws away from the window. Obviously, he would have been accused of apathy if he had not tried to find out if her wife were okay, because all he knew was that she had gone downstairs to answer the door that late at night.

117. Women's higher intuition leads to other obstacles too. First, it makes them hasty and adamant in their judgments. Second, it increases their tendency to see and feel things without too much communication. Often they believe they can somehow read their husbands' minds and detect the hidden clues in their conversations. They also assume that their husbands have the same level of intuition to understand their wishes without communicating the ideas to them clearly. They say something and expect their husbands to read between the lines and grasp their intentions. Then they

get surprised and frustrated when their husbands do not comprehend their messages. Often they actually believe that their husbands have gotten the message, but are refusing to accept it or do something about it. Women believe that men are (or should be) as careful and intuitive as they are. They do not recognize that men's lower intuitiveness cannot be helped. Besides, men's logic dictates their need for clear communication instead of guessing the meaning of a vague message.

118. Overall, women do not believe in, and actually resist, an open and precise communication, maybe because they feel their husbands are not listening, anyway, or are not interested. However, women have also become oversensitive and react harshly when men cannot understand their vague messages. As noted above, women's intuition is filling the gap that hinders men's understanding of a message without full communication. Men require clarity and women resist it since they find it unnecessary and unromantic, or they stay vague merely out of spite occasionally too. They simply expect their husbands to understand their meanings and intentions. For example, a husband was complaining to the author that whenever his wife realized her mistake, she only tried to make up for it by preparing his favourite meal, buying him a pair of socks, or making some kind of an indirect gesture of these natures. However, she never apologized directly or admitted that she had made a mistake. She simply expected to get the matter resolved without acknowledging the problem or discussing it. He said that, without an open discussion about the problem and a sincere apology, the matter never got resolved in his mind and his wounds never healed. Actually, he considered his wife's behaviour (i.e., the gesture of buying him a present or

cooking a fine meal) another type of manipulation and rising arrogance.

119. Couples are unaware of the hurdles of finding a new companion after getting out of their existing relationships. They are naïvely too optimistic about their chances of finding a reasonable match, even in their older ages. This is in particular difficult for women who are seeking men of higher qualities after their past relationships fail. Accordingly, couples' problems and frustrations would keep increasing in their second and third relationships. The only exception is when one or both partners become somewhat passive in their new relationship.

120. Many couples prefer to deal with the imperfections of their existing relationships rather than a new one. This is because they get used to its flaws and their partners' shortfalls after many years of sharing both good memories and life's hardships together. They learn to bear their relationship flaws by always recalling its merits. They admit that both partners in almost all relationships are most likely annoyed by each other's quirks. They feel that bearing the imperfections of their existing relationship is easier than learning about, and accepting, the new imperfections of a stranger (a new companion) all of a sudden. Men are particularly lazy, too, to go through the hassle of finding a new companion if the existing relationship is not too bad.

121. People usually expect peace in a new relationship after tolerating their previous partners' imperfections. For men especially, staying lonely seems preferable to living with a person who brings different kinds of idiosyncrasies and childish demands. People hate learning new stuff and adjusting, especially at the later stages of their lives. With old age, they need less sex and usually have less patience or

incentives, anyway, while getting more grouchy and demanding too.

122. We seek relationships to relieve our loneliness, but soon find out the absurdity of our dreams and efforts, because relationships actually make us feel the ultimate depth of loneliness and helplessness.

123. Everybody is getting more defensive in their interactions with others due to their experiences, rising gender differences, and the increasing level of aggressiveness in society. This is, of course, an added psychological pressure in relationships. We speak with people and our partners with apprehension (superficially), in order to not trigger their defence mechanisms and start an argument. This situation keeps relationships too edgy and unnatural. At the same time, people are also becoming more aggressive and offensive in order to counterbalance their partners' assertiveness; as the saying goes: the best defence is offence.

124. Often relationships get into trouble when partners are unhappy with themselves and the life they are leading. Therefore, they depress their partners with their attitude too. Often they blame their partners for their own career failures, unhappiness, boredom, or unfulfilled dreams. Sometimes they nag at each other to conceal their own shortfalls, e.g., in socializing. Then they gradually hate each other because they believe that their partner is in fact responsible for their unhappiness.

125. Partners waste a lot of time and energy on faultfinding and blaming each other supposedly for the sake of improving their relationship.

126. In fact, coupled can save their relationships if only they realized that in the end it does not matter whose fault the

problems are as long as those problems remain irreconcilable.

127. The bottom line is that couples must either find mutually agreeable solutions (a suitable relationship model) to relate somehow or separate. When relationship problems go beyond certain levels, the only solution is to find ways of relating (living together) passively at a lower level of the relationship tree (model), and stop trying to solve the problems per se. Problems are often unsolvable, because they are caused by irreversible idiosyncrasies of partners. We humans have proven that not even our logic and common sense can help us solve our personal or social (including economic and political) problems.

128. The gender struggles to reach some illusory balance of power and equality is continuing at many levels, and the situation would most likely get out of hand in the future, with global destructive outcomes.

129. What works for women in a relationship does not work for men anymore, and vice versa. In particular, men and women mistrust the opposite genders much more than their own. The increasing same-sex relationships might be partly due to the fact that they get along better.

130. In all, it appears that we are reaching an era where men can no longer be what women want (in terms of character) and vice versa.

131. We have difficulty learning from our mistakes and from the pains that our relationships are causing us. We prefer to suffer than change our perspective about the inherent limitations of relationships, especially within the context of the existing lifestyles. Accordingly, it would be hard for the controversial messages of this book to find popularity amidst the mass of beautifully packaged messages (and so-

cial values) promising prosperity and happiness to every-body.

132. One of the main goals of a relationship framework is to bring *objectivity* back into relationships. However, a main hurdle is selling the idea of objectivity to women who are used to dealing with issues intuitively, and to men whose sense of logic has already made them dogmatic.

133. Nonetheless, society must gradually propagate the guide-lines of a relationship framework. A more logical atmos-phere must replace gender struggles for superiority. Reach-ing a balance of power and identity would require some form of objectivity eventually. Otherwise, chaos would bring family relationships to a halt.

134. A puzzling point is, 'What kind of a partner are couples looking for when they insist on breaking each other's pride, mainly by competing with each other relentlessly?' In par-ticular, a relevant question is, "Whether women can ever find submissive men attractive and trustworthy at all?" How could women enjoy or respect weak men?

135. Another major conflict is emerging: Couples are expecting their partners to be strong, competitive, and assertive out-side the house to maximize families' welfare, but be sub-missive and passive at home to accommodate them.

136. The emerging trends in society, especially couples' needs for individuality and independence, are irreversible. And people's psychological attributes cannot be changed either. Therefore, the only solution for our relationships is to find new mechanisms and relationship principles to match our new needs.

137. In addition, couples should get more serious about modify-ing their mindsets and viewing relationships in a new per-

spective. They should do so for increasing their chances of building a reliable relationship.

138. Partners' drive for independence leads to more distance between them if they have not chosen a proper relationship model or understand the implications of being tactful in their relationship. Working within a relationship framework, while advocating partners' independence, rectifies this problem largely. Couples learn to respect and deal with their partners' need for independence and view 'independence' as a major requirement of teamwork. Meanwhile, more detailed mechanisms of teamwork must be developed too.

139. The way we behave nowadays, hardly can anybody find his or her soul mate. Even if we happen to find them by accident, we just keep losing them due to our phony personalities and ideologies, not to mention our idiotic games and Ego. It is interesting that even couples with similar values, lifestyle, and priorities keep rejecting one another since they do not give themselves a chance to relate authentically and choose a proper relationship model.

140. Some couples indeed find their soul mates, but lose them when their own oversensitivity gives them wrong impressions about the health of their relationship and the purpose of relationships in general. They lose their partners due to their fantasies, such as a better life with a different partner, love, money, etc. High expectations and misperceptions are making couples lose the soul mates they have already found.

141. Partners get too intimate too early as a sign of love, trust, and loyalty, instead of proving all of these high qualities gradually through real actions and right attitude. Often, partners actually try to manipulate each other by showing

off a polished image of themselves. Nevertheless, statistics show that most couples end up losing their love, trust, and loyalty in their relationships.

142. Partners try to exploit each other (knowingly or inadvertently) by *activating their MLove to fake SLove to get ELove.*

143. People assume they are (or can be) loving, trustworthy, or loyal. However, all evidences indicate that humans are impure by nature, and then environment makes them even more cruel and aggressive.

144. Relationships suffer from humans' inherent defects more than anything else, while gender differences exacerbate the problems. Some artificial expressions of passion, as a result of attraction or other needs of partners, do not change their true nature as humans with all their inherent defects and all kinds of gender quarrels.

145. Our rampant relationship issues are causing more mistrust amongst youth. Thus, each generation is causing more damages for the relationships of the future generations. We are making our children more sceptical about marriage and less prepared to deal with its requirements, especially its most likely consequence, i.e., separation.

146. Accordingly, gender differences and quarrels are leading to deeper suspicions for every generation about the opposite sex.

147. Driven by the recent popular ideologies, including positive thinking slogans, people like to believe that life is beautiful and that happiness is within reach. Yet, most prominent philosophies and our personal experiences indicate the opposite: That life is nothing but a place for suffering and paying for our past or present sins. The point is that our idealism and search for this phantom happiness are mis-

leading many couples; they just put too much demand on each other recklessly and then finally separate.

148. It is a pity that our misguided perceptions stop us from taking advantage of our only opportunity to suffer less in this world: That is, by bringing more objectivity into our relationships and enjoying one another, instead of arguing about our inconsequential needs and obsessions, especially this illusive 'happiness.' We are actually proving the philosophers right about life being only a place for suffering. Most ironically, we suffer from our relationships (or lack of them) due to our own naïve expectations and games.

149. Being optimistic and positive about life are useful tools. However, when they cause gross misperceptions and raise our naïve expectations, e.g., for more love or a better partner, they must be construed as another cause of partners' confusion and relationship failures.

150. The bottom line is that if positive thinking and 'living in the now' schemes worked, by now everybody would have joined in to reap their rewards. Everybody would have benefited from these magical cures by now and we could see all those happy faces around us. However, all we see is more depression, desperation, gender quarrels, and relationship failures. We need the highest level of antidepressants to help us continue living with less suffering. If these schemes worked, relationship problems had disappeared and everybody was living happily with their soul mates. Instead, we see more unrealizable expectations, self-pity, and quarrels.

151. Many people are edgy these days because their positive thinking alone, even when they combine it with a great deal of personal efforts, does not seem to get them anywhere. They still lose their companions to the phony life

philosophies that are misleading people, and they still lose their life savings in financial markets because of other people's greed or incompetence.

152. Many philosophers suggest that life cannot be a happy affair, because the minute we have nothing to do, and can supposedly enjoy life, we get bored. So we look for adventure, work, or a new companion to rejuvenate our lives. However, they all make us suffer, too, especially our relationships.

153. In all, we struggle all our lives to find something creative to do or a worthy companion to give us some moments of happiness. Some spiritualists, of course, believe that we could help ourselves a little if we learned to be a better human being and stayed content, which is a tough mission for most of us.

154. Nowadays, being a good human does not always pay off anyway. He/she is often perceived as a weak and passive individual and not taken seriously. It might not help (actually damage) his/her relationship, anyway, if his/her partner is not an equally good human being. Therefore, being a good person may not be necessarily useful for drawing other people's compassion or achieving tangible benefits.

155. The only benefit of being good is to mitigate our own suffering and possibly get a better chance to relate to our partners unselfishly. This a grand incentive, though, if we learn to be a bit wiser.

156. Along with our personal efforts to become a better human and partner, we must consider a wide range of radical changes in our mentality as well as social setting to make our relationships more constructive.

CHAPTER EIGHT
Gender Sensitive Personal Needs

HUMAN qualities, quirks, and social setting cause a large variety of dilemmas and obstacles in relationships as discussed in the previous chapters. Ironically, the roots of these obstacles and the repercussions of gender differences are all related to our crude personal needs and perceptions, as they obscure the objectives of relationships. In particular, realizing the role of the following ten personal needs through some minimal self-awareness can improve our relationships tremendously:

1. Dependence
2. Independence
3. Happiness
4. Love
5. Sex
6. Equality
7. Individualism
8. Fairness
9. Control
10. Domination

Most of the above noted needs sound logical expectations for every healthy person living in a modern society. We strive to satisfy these needs in order to maximize the value of our lives or defend ourselves against the widespread evil in society. However, deep emotional conflicts arise and many obstacles cripple relationships when the couples' struggle for the same things, e.g., happiness, affects their views of their partners and the health of their relationships. The above ten personal needs are particularly gender sensitive in the way they affect partners' perceptions of, and interactions with, the opposite gender.

Needs for Dependence and Independence

We face many inner conflicts while trying to develop our character. They make us think and behave in certain bizarre ways. We learn how to deal with many of these conflicts eventually and some of them become irrelevant when we move on to the next stages of our lives. However, one particular conflict stays with us for the rest of our lives. This persistent conflict arises when our two fundamental needs for dependence and independence keep clashing constantly in our mind. These inherent needs play a major role in our lives, sometimes more prominently than any single need that humans usually have. In fact, any one of our needs often remains at the mercy of our needs for dependence and independence. Our needs are often reinforced or dampened only based on our prominent need for independence (or dependence) regardless of the consequences. For example, our pride (a symptom of independence) often defies any single need, even the need for food or survival. We go on hunger strike sometimes. In this sense, pride finds urgency even ahead of our basic needs.

On the other hand, our need for dependence, e.g., the need for passion and a companion, might supersede our need for food or even breathing. We might prefer to die when loneliness is crippling our existence and mind. The point of interest here is that our personal needs for dependence and independence are overwhelming and they cause deep conflicts for us too. However, more importantly, partners' inner conflicts due to these needs infect their relationship severely. In particular, the new social setting is affecting genders differently in terms of their needs for dependence and independence as discussed in Chapter Three. Nonetheless, only by understanding the intricacy of these needs we might learn to relate to our partners. We must realize that both partners' drives for the same needs (especially dependence and independence) must somehow coincide or we just keep widening the gender gap, in practice and in terms of gender mentalities.

The conflicting nature of gender needs for dependence and independence was discussed in the previous chapters, including points 5-6 on pages 29-30 and points 9-10 on pages 38-39. The unique ways partners perceive and attend to these needs induce wider gender conflicts and more quarrels. Therefore, it is useful to understand these personal needs in some detail.

At adolescence, we get ready to gain our independence from family and their lifestyle. We begin to develop our own thoughts and preferences. We strive to show off our individualism and freedom through all types of rebellions and exaggerated expressions with our opinions, appearance, attire, etc. Meanwhile, some weird feelings for dependence begin to creep into our heads sneakily. We feel the need to belong to groups of friends, be accepted by others, be loved by a girlfriend or boyfriend, and fit within many features of social living (not to mention drugs, alcohol, and cigarettes). As we proceed through life, the number of dependencies piles up, while, at the same time, we struggle to develop our unique identity and independence. We get frustrated when our independence is constantly threatened by our need for dependence on other people and society. We feel our independence invaded and we hate those who are doing it.

When we get the opportunity of entering a relationship, we realize the need to give up some of our autonomy for the benefits of companionship. We may find this trade-off equitable initially. However, we find it humiliating when even small conflicts make us doubt our identity, the purpose of our relationships, and the value of our sacrifices. We hate the way our partner is squashing our independence. The longer we stay in a relationship, the larger the level of personal conflict between dependence and independence gets, and the more pressure is put on the relationship.

Especially, with the social emphasis on individualism and independence nowadays, our inner conflict due to our needs for both dependence and independence has become too prominent. We try to create some level of balance between our needs for dependence and independence in order to make our relationships manageable in societies that are satiated with slogans of personal identity and individualism. Creating and maintaining this balance is tough, even if such a balance could be found. Most couples have difficulty in this area.

Yet, a tougher inner conflict resides even deeper in our psyche. This conflict stems from the fact that many people seek dependence obsessively because of their prominent insecurities and need for a companion. 'Need for a companion' is a strong, complex personal need that expands across all levels of human needs. Companionship satisfies our basic, medium, and high level needs. Most of us seek compassion and a companion almost more than anything else. Although we acknowledge the need for creating a practical balance between independence and dependence, we might be a very needy person inherently. We might prefer to depend totally on our partners. We want to depend on her/him to provide the compassion and passion that we crave. We might even need someone to lead us through life. This is a much higher level of dependence than a normal person with logical balance (between dependence and independence) needs. Meanwhile, we do not want to show our neediness to our partner, especially if he/she is not as needy as we are. Therefore, while one partner insists on creating a workable balance for partners' independence, the other partner hides his/her need for more (or total) dependence. Yet, he/she hopes all along that his/her obsessive (but unexpressed) need for dependence is understood. Another way of stating this condition is that most individuals' need for ELove has increased irrationally in recent decades, but they hate to admit it. Their Egos stop them from expressing their true need for all that extra attention and compassion, mostly because it is not fashionable to show their vulnerabilities and inability to be independent.

In all, even a moderate drive for independence requires (and leads to) a lot of isolation and self-reliance, which only few can manage realistically. Dependence, on the other hand, is mostly synonymous with compassion and a willingness to pay a price for it. We all value compassion a lot. We feel the need for dependence on another individual and society, because we doubt our ability to survive as an independent person. Some of us need dependency to another person—a lover perhaps—more urgently in order to validate our identity and existence. Yet, our partners and society do not have the capacity to cope with our need for dependence. In most cases, they actually ridicule and take advantage of our perceived weakness, i.e., our inability to be independent. However, even for people seeking dependence obsessively, their need for independence emerges quite regularly too. Even this group's need for dependence is not absolute and permanent. It continues to remain an unmanageable urge.

The matter gets fully out of hand when we pretend to be more independent than we really feel we are, or can handle. Most of us are trained nowadays to insist on our individuality and independence. That is how we believe we can assert ourselves and show our identity. We learn to play all kinds of roles and games to prove our independence and strong identity. However, as we engage in these types of exaggerations, to prove our needlessness, we place a higher pressure on our psyche to set a fake balance between our needs for dependence and independence. We lose touch with reality and our true needs. We are in effect imposing another set of artificial needs on ourselves that are unachievable. At the same time, we are depriving ourselves from fulfilling our need for dependence. These artificial needs and situations cause more inner conflicts and psychological damages. They widen the gender gap and lead to futile clashes with our partners too. We become aggressive in order to show assertiveness, mostly because we do not know the delicate art of assertiveness. In most situations, assertiveness might not even be in our nature anyway. We are fighting our own natural urges to become somebody else. We play the role of an independent person with some imaginary identity, but unfulfilled. This kind of confusion causes identity crisis, of course, and often we feel this deficiency ourselves too. Yet, we keep seeking independence, anyway, because we are brainwashed to play those roles; to fight for our individuality and identity no matter what. Our artificial need to show off our independence, as a symbol of freedom and identity, has in effect become counter productive for both our individuality and relationships.

Conversely, many people have become too submissive and dependent upon their relationships. They accept all kinds of humiliations and intimidation, including their partners' infidelity. Only a few decades ago, infidelity was a taboo and led to an automatic divorce. Not anymore! Yet, even these people, with high dependence orientation and a submissive attitude, have difficulty sustaining their relationships. Their sacrifices go unnoticed and they lose their relationships unexpectedly. Some of these people might eventually learn that it is impossible to depend on others, even their partners. To survive in their relationships without getting hurt too much, they eventually learn to play the role of an independent person with a strong identity. They just have to. They are forced to behave that way. The bottom line is that partners' need for dependence is undervalued at so many levels by our new lifestyles, values, and social pressures. It is trendy to show one's aptitude for individualism. Therefore, people pretend to be independent in order to fit and survive. They are forced into this position (seeking independence) to defend themselves and fit. However, of course, they remain inherently a dependent, depressed person.

Obviously, the smart thing nowadays is to not depend on others or their words. They simply cannot deliver because of the limitations in their own lives and psyche, and not necessarily out of spite. In fact, beyond people's *instinctual urge* for independence, three other reasons make people struggle for independence: (1) they have become too obsessed with their need for expressing individualism and asserting their identity, (2) they must strive to cope with social norms and being accepted, and (3) they eventually learn they cannot depend on others.

Another dependence-independence paradox happens in relationships when partners try to acquire more independence for themselves, but want to maximize their partners' neediness to them. They strive to gain more power in their relationships by dominating their partners. Thus, an ongoing struggle continues between partners to maintain a balance of power in order to stop the other from dominating them. Everybody likes more independence for themselves, but much less for their partners. Men were more domineering in the past, but the trend is reversing in the new era due to women's struggle to assert themselves. Nonetheless, the power struggle for domination is causing major conflicts in relationships nowadays. Instead of creating a relaxed environment, partners' quarrels to maintain 'the needed balance' lead to frictions, mistrust, miscommunications, and misperceptions.

In all, a bizarre trend is emerging as a result of couples' struggle to cope with their needs for dependence and independence: Some couples seek separation with the slightest inconvenience in their relationships (high need for independence and individualism); and some couples accept abuse and adultery as they are too apprehensive about loneliness and isolation (high need for dependence and compassion). These prevalent extremes show the extent of value changes in new societies. They show the extreme imbalance between our needs for independence and dependence, and a general confusion about the role of relationships as an important social concept. A major conclusion is that we are not as strong as we often wish, or pretend, to be in our exaggerated show of independence and individualism. We are not equipped to create a reasonable balance between our needs for dependence and independence in our relationships either. Therefore, the question is whether a framework can be developed and used by couples to reconcile their conflicting urges for dependence and independence in relationships.

The contentious issues concerning our personal needs for dependence and independence are summarized below:

1. We are not quite conscious of our conflicting needs for dependence and independence. Nor are we aware of the high repercussions of this conflict for us, our relationships, and society in general.

2. We do not know how to define or judge our personal needs for independence and dependence. We do not know how to be independent or dependent when we go about satisfying these needs alternately on a regular basis. Some people pretend to be independent and needless when deep down their need for dependence is overwhelming. And some people damage their identity when they become submissive.

3. We play the kind of roles that others suggest, usually with the highest emphasis on independence, since we do not know how to set and keep a practical balance between our conflicting needs for independence and dependence. Yet, everybody has a different balance of needs for independence and dependence according to his/her personality. Ignoring one's particular needs (for dependence and independence) and sticking to some fake balance creates confusion and frustration.

4. Partners do not know how to discuss and match their needs for dependence and independence—mostly because it might require some kind of compromise, which would be against their presumed identity and independence.

Therefore, they end up arguing about every detail or decision.

5. Without knowing about our needs for independence and dependence and the balance most suitable for us, we expect our partners to behave as if they did know what the right balance should be. For example, we expect them to respect our independence when we suddenly feel it is time for us to be independent; we ask for a vaster boundary. And then we expect them to be compassionate and caring as soon as we need their attention to satisfy our need for dependence (ELove).

6. We turn off our partners with our exaggerated show of independence and needlessness. And we confuse them with our silly roles and games to enforce our alternating needs for dependence and independence. These erratic interactions make it difficult for partners to relate to each other. Meanwhile, power struggles to dominate our partners, and enforce our gender identities, postpone the matter of finding the right balance (between dependence and independence). Only arrogance and phoniness prevail in this kind of environment. All these conditions hinder the task of bringing objectivity and peace into relationships.

7. As social complexity and the public's intelligence increase every year, people's demands for both independence and dependence will rise. They seek more independence because society pushes them to express themselves, and prove their identity, more explicitly. However, they also seek more dependence (need for a compassionate companion) because of the increased level of stress in their daily lives and the overall sense of loneliness. Therefore, instead of balancing their needs for de-

pendence and independence, people struggle even more with their anxiety and inner conflicts.

8. The topics covered in this book demonstrate how the increased imbalance (between our needs for independence and dependence) is forced upon us due to our lifestyles and mentalities. Gender differences and quarrels will increase and relationships will become more instable in the future, while their longevity will continue to decline too.

9. The inner conflict due to dependence/independence imbalance affects our moods randomly, usually at worst situations, e.g., when our partner is angry and pushing our nerves. We react harshly because the balance we had presumably imposed for our needs for independence and dependence is threatened. Our partners react harshly, too, for the same reasons—not out of spite perhaps, but only as a by-product of chemical and mental reactions in their bodies. This inner conflict seems to be triggered when we get into arguments with our partners. However, in reality, it is an ongoing struggle within us causing all sorts of insecurity and doubts about our identity.

10. A person's needs for dependence/independence are not complementary (or contradictory). It is quite likely that his/her needs for both dependence and independence are high or low. In such cases, creating a balance between partners' dependence/independence is even more difficult. They are usually less-balanced persons to begin with.

To mitigate their inner conflict, each partner in a relationship should deal with their dilemma of dependence versus independence in three distinct ways as follows:

1. He/she should initially try to establish his/her realistic needs for dependence and independence, based on his/her personality alone, without considering any compromises necessary for being in any serious relationship with a partner. The idea is to establish one's true temperament and needs regardless of social pressures for independence or the level of compromise needed in a relationship.

2. He/she should establish the levels of dependency/ independency that he/she can envision for his/her partner. Usually people dislike partners who seek too much independence. However, more crucial than this case is when a person is unprepared (perhaps psychologically) or unwilling to be responsible for a partner who requires too much dependence (emotionally or financially). Therefore, he/she should figure out his/her potential partner's inclination for dependence/ independence realistically before committing him/herself to any partnership.

3. Together with his/her potential partner, they should establish the kind of dependency/independency balance they require in their relationship and then choose the right relationship model for them. This balance should fit the other two above decisions that each partner must make personally, then they choose the right relationship model.

Need for Happiness

Happiness is a myth all by itself, but finding it in relationships is even more idealistic. We have difficulty even defining it because it is not a stable state or experience. Yet, we like to perceive it as a lasting state of joy and tranquility, which we also expect to result from our endless materialistic desires, greed, and competition. This is a major conflict already. We want happiness to fit our contaminated lifestyles, instead of a lifestyle that could induce peace of mind as the closest state of happiness. We forget that any chance for happiness requires a drastic change of personal lifestyle (mainly toward selflessness), which only a few of us might eventually find the courage to adopt.

Nevertheless, partners expect each other and their relationship to satisfy their illusory perceptions of happiness, including their egotistical and materialistic needs, pleasure, sexuality, and lasting tranquility. This expectation is actually one major cause of relationship breakdowns. Partners deprive themselves from the basic privileges of relationships because they believe relationships are meant to bring them happiness. They cause themselves more pain with their obsession for happiness through relationships. We have brought this ironic condition upon ourselves in recent decades. Instead of learning selflessness and contentment, partners try to strengthen their identities in relationships through arrogance, and then expect happiness too. In that sense, relationships create the best setting for the wickedest aspects of human nature to erupt and cause suffering and depression rather than happiness.

In fact, human nature does not support happiness and tranquility due to humans' innate urges for challenge, power, controversy, domination, competition, greed, struggle for survival, etc. Anger, hatred, jealousy, spite, and aggressiveness come to us so naturally, but we must try really hard to be honest, compassionate, sincere, and all the other good stuff required for attaining happiness. Life is not a happy journey either. Our occasional taste of happiness and tranquility soon dissolves as new dilemmas and disappointments overwhelm us. Therefore, as the first step toward tranquility, and also improving our relationships, we must learn that happiness is a myth and not a stable state.

As another misperception, most of us mistake pleasures (especially sexuality) with happiness, or assume that more pleasures lead to happiness. So, most relationships become instable soon enough, only because they fail to satisfy our fantastic appetite for happiness through sexuality. Of course, we cannot avoid the impression that companionship can fulfil a large number of our personal needs. However, depending on others or relationships to satisfy our personal needs and bring us happiness is naïve and the leading cause of our suffering. Any chance for tasting this elusive happiness is to seek it within ourselves according to our mental capacity and awareness. Most importantly, we must relieve our relationships from our demands to bring us happiness.

Happiness is a complex topic for discussion, especially within the context of our crooked social values. Many books are written on this topic and maybe another one is due to explain the connection between happiness and relationships in more details than are possible in this book. The natural conclusion in most 'happiness' books is that it may be found only inside a person and he/she needs a special mindset to understand and reach that state. This is what this author advocates as well with an emphasis on becoming better humans through personal awareness, to contact our spirit and become needless about many artificial facets of life in the new era. However, this book also emphasizes on staying practical and understanding our humanistic limitations, which hinder our efforts to be content and a better person. A great collection of happiness definitions can be found in *Happiness*, Perennial Books, 2014.

Some books (quoting philosophers, Buddhism, and the Dalai Lama) suggest that the purpose of life is to find happiness. This notion seems rather too simplistic, because life does not have a purpose by itself and humans have many other ambitions besides happiness. The purpose of life (in the context of creation) is neither to spread happiness nor to create good human beings. Happiness is not even the purpose of one's life (regardless of the purpose of the universe). Life is merely a collection of events and moments that transpires in people's lives according to natural laws and chances and affects them based on their cognition (i.e., beliefs, awareness, intelligence, etc.). We all prefer happiness because suffering hurts, and not because it is the purpose of life. We have many higher ambitions in life that we often pursue with greater passion than our desire for happiness or even pleasures, e.g., need for love, power, or recognition. Most of us just cannot sit idle and be happy with our contentment. We resent boredom and we want more adventures even if they cause suffering. We want to be loved even though it often leads to disappointment and pain. The point is that we are not born to be happy or good humans and these are not the purposes of life. We want to become better human beings to soothe our hurts, release tension, or because we sometimes prefer (or like to pretend) to be at peace with our surroundings and ourselves. Happiness and goodness are the probable outcomes of our personal choices to set the right balance between our ambitions and contentment. Life does not have any particular meaning, nor is it about anything in particular. Even if life is about something or has a meaning, God has not yet revealed it to us through His prophets, nor has He given us enough intelligence to figure it out personally.

The slogan 'life is for the purpose of happiness' is in fact causing more suffering than guiding people toward happiness. The reason is that it makes people believe that such a myth (happiness) actually exists, and that the reason they cannot grasp it is due to their stupidity or relationships. They feel incompetent and frustrated. They leave their relationships prematurely or seek all kinds of pleasures and sexuality to attain the purpose of life, i.e., happiness. But then, they feel even more empty and lost.

Most importantly, life is not for the purpose of getting hung-up over a mythical concept like happiness and causing extra suffering for ourselves and our marriage partners. Ninety-nine percent of us cannot find that elusive happiness. The one percent who claims to have found it, like monks and sages, must make many sacrifices, limit their social activities, and accept celibacy and suffering in order to maintain their state of contentment, which they call happiness. It seems that happiness has a lot to do with selflessness, meditation, celibacy, and absorbing sufferings. However, by nature, most of us are selfish, and like our sexuality and pleasures a lot, which would accordingly lead to unhappiness. How many of us are willing to be celibate, limit our pleasures and social lives, and welcome sufferings to reach the height of enlightenment (for happiness)? We have to really force ourselves to fulfil most of these requirements, which shows happiness can never be a natural pursuit of humans, especially in our materialistic world. Accordingly, the purpose of our existence is not to seek happiness, as the Dalai Lama says, because we humans are not prepared to pay the price for it and we are not made for it. Seeking happiness might be a wrong strategy for many of us indeed, as it appears to be against our nature. We must think and act within our natural capacities, while aiming to be better human beings too. In particular, blaming our relationships and partners for not inducing the happiness that we cannot find anywhere else on our own is a silly attitude prevalent in society nowadays.

The fact that we crave happiness in vain reveals our inner turmoil and inability to define our existence in simpler terms personally. The fact that we have to try so hard to become better persons shows that humans are not pure by nature. It also reveals our stubbornness to accept our inherent debility as humans. On the other hand, acknowledging our impurity could motivate us to overcome our Egos and try harder to grasp the meaning and process of becoming a better human; not merely because it would be a social ideal, but because it would make us happier at the end. The simple fact that the Ego is an inherent part of the human psyche is enough to cause human bias, selfishness, hypocrisy, and hundreds of other flaws. The fact that we are so greedy and competitive, and the way we love capitalism, materialism, and pleasures show that we are impure by nature. The fact that Christians believe Jesus died because of their sins—and similar beliefs in other religions—shows humans' tendency to sin. The fact that so many relationships fail nowadays, and the way partners treat each other like dirt at the time of separation, show their impurity. It also shows people's inability to get along and show compassion. The fact that we must constantly go for confessions and repentance, to cleanse our souls, is another clue about our impurity. The fact that we do good things and charity as well (often for self-serving purposes, to clean our conscience, or for pretension) does not wash all other negative tendencies that exist in human nature.

The success of a relationship depends on the goodness of its partners. However, individuals' characteristics, actions, and nature indicate that the chance of creating even a small society of pure humans is slim, because they would not be left alone to choose and live as they like. In fact, it is easier to prove that humans become more arrogant and unreliable as time goes by and gender differences increase too. Thus, it becomes harder for people (especially opposite genders) to get along in relationships and communities and grasp happiness. Developing a pure man within the crooked value systems of modern society simply appears like a funny concept. It sounds like a plan to nurture edible fish in a tainted swamp. With the speed we are destroying the environment, where nature is supposed to flourish itself and embrace us too, how could a puritan emerge? How can anybody find happiness within this social chaos?

Need for Love

In the recent decades, couples have suddenly become too romantic, but also too antagonistic. Everybody, especially women, believe that love should be the foundation of relationships. In this sense, life has become a big theatre. Everybody tries to be romantic. And they expect their partners to be equally good in romance, too, as a test of their commitment. Yet, they retaliate harshly, and show their evil sides, when love fades away—which happens regularly in most relationships. They turn separation into such a calamity when they realize that their supposedly initial love had been a farce. They make life hell for themselves and their partners because love has evaporated (if there had been any real love to begin with). Now couples turn into ferocious adversaries accusing each other of lying about their love promises at the outset. They curse their partners for not loving them anymore, as if love were something to force upon oneself and not a natural phenomenon. They find their partners responsible for the lost love, even if they are the ones feeling out of love. Actually, they often blame their partners for making them fall out of love. They accuse their partners of having killed their love.

They also blame them for their loss of youth. These past lovers now suddenly view each other as criminals deserving a severe punishment, including a difficult and costly separation. The penalty for falling out of love is too horrendous nowadays. Therefore, some people continue to play the role of a romantic fool to keep the situation under control. They accept the humiliation of submitting to the whims of their spouses to stop their whining, and because the penalties, financially and emotionally, for ending relationships are too high.

As explained in Chapter Three, the gender gap regarding love is rather wide. First, women have a higher aptitude for, and misperceptions about, all three types of love, i.e., Slove, Elove, and Mlove compared with men. This difference causes many misunderstanding and gender quarrels. Second, while women would like to use love as a measure for relationship success, men are losing their trust in love, especially since they are instinctually and culturally less inclined to be romantic and sensitive enough for women's liking. Men and women are so incompatible in general that when, by chance, they match and really love one another for a long time, it appears like a magical and spiritual sensation beyond our normal (expected) worldly experiences. It is such an odd event and coincidence. And still we are too naïve to believe it should happen to all of us and thus we pursue it like a reasonable expectation.

Almost everybody finally admits that love, in the sense they had initially imagined it, is a transitory state. Then they may decide that the option of staying in loveless relationships, against their convictions, is preferable to loneliness or high penalties of separation. However, they now do not know how to handle a relationship that is not defined by love. They believe their relationship has failed and has no value. Some may

seek love in another person's arms; to find the love they believe they deserve.

Everybody believes s/he deserves love and must find it
somehow. However, we all ignore a simple fact about the
meaning of love: That the more one seeks SLove, the more
one must be honest and sincere in character. Yet, it is becoming more difficult to be honest and sincere nowadays, because
of all the games introduced in relationships. Of course, we
imagine that we can hide our insincerity, mistrust, and dishon-
esty from the rest of the world. However, this mentality only
shows our arrogance and trust in Model to bail us out. The
good news is that people can largely see each other's true nature despite all the elaborate games they play to portray a false
personality of themselves and to conceal their calculating nature. In all, the games and retaliation schemes in relationships
show how ridiculous the idea of measuring the strength of our
relationships by love is. We just ignore all these contradictions
and keep looking for SLove in such a contaminated environment.

In such convoluted social setting, the matter of resolving
our relationship conundrums have become too complex too.
On the one hand, getting out of our relationships proves ex-
cruciating, in terms of the hardships imposed by our partners
and society (the judicial system in particular). On the other
hand, many couples are frustrated and confused, nowadays,
because they feel trapped in their loveless (usually hostile)
relationships. The situation is in particular stressful for persons
who truly believe that love is the essence of relationships.
Even worse, many couples have to continue playing some
phony roles that marriage counsellors recommend in order to
save their relationships.

Our present mindset reflects our lack of clarity about the nature of love and its role in relationships. We insist that relationships, and their survival, must be justified and driven by love. In the contemporary definition of relationships, our culture permeates many invalid myths. We believe that:

- Love is the test of success for relationships.
- Love lasts forever.
- Love makes a relationship last forever.
- Relationships must be validated by love.
- Relationships thrive on love.
- Anybody considering a serious relationship should and would find a person to exchange love with each other.
- Expressing love regularly guarantees the success of relationships.
- Love is a common phenomenon that everyone understands and is capable of delivering.
- Love is a common commodity that everyone must find and enjoy in his/her life.
- When there is love, relationship problems are rare and manageable.
- Love overcomes all the relationship problems.
- Partners have control over their feelings to love each other forever.
- Etc.

These myths are furthest from the nature of relationships in the new era. Love does not have the meaning or the power stipulated in the above myths. Nor do relationships necessarily last longer if partners start their relationships mostly based on the strength of their love. We are not learning any lesson from the fact that almost all relationships in the modern world have started based on *some kind of love* and they still keep failing miserably. It is amazing.

The scientific evidence about the role of human hormones on our behaviour is another proof of our misperception about the power of love. In particular, our hormones do not support the idea of monogamy in humans. Many studies have also shown that our infatuation and love dies within six months to two years. More details about the effect of human hormones can be found in other relationship books by this author.

Maybe it is all right to seek love so eagerly. However, we should also remember the nature of love in general as well as the chaotic nature of relationships in the new era. We should do so to be prepared for the consequences of our futile search for love or even finding it. We should indeed concentrate on developing our Self (selflessness) instead of indulging ourselves with more ELove and phony lovers. Besides, SLove happens by accident and not active search.

Another cause for misperception in relationships is that partners use love as another yardstick for measuring equality. That is, they expect their partners to love them as much as they think (or pretend) they love their partners. They demand love-equality to ensure the fairness of their relationships. Obviously, love-equality is a symptom of the general equality craze in society. People believe that love is a spiritual feeling (Self driven), but then make it totally conditional on their partners' ability to love them equally. With their demands for ELove and equality, they simply expose their selfishness (instead of selflessness) and destroy their chances to relax and relate naturally.

Couples' perception and expression of love are obviously not SLove as long as they insist on love equality. It is even more bizarre when they often retaliate harshly when they do not perceive the love they get adequate. How can this attitude have any trace of SLove in it? It is at best only a Model driven love (where partners try to play the role of lovers), without any sense of selflessness (needlessness for equality). This is clearly an example of partners' increasing confusion every day about their perceptions of love, which then leads to more expectations from relationships. The need for equality has become such an imposing social phenomenon that it has infected even our love affairs. We are less interested in figuring out how our partners' integrity may qualify them as our soul mates. Nobody knows what the characteristics of a soul mate should be. Rather, we insist on measuring, in greatest accuracy, the equality (as well as the intensity) of the love our partners can show, which we continue to doubt anyway.

While equality, in the sense of *fairness,* is the foundation of our democratic society, it has turned into a socio-political platform to further spread our demented social values. The term 'equality' is somewhat misused inadvertently to express our repressed anxieties, which then leads to creation of new expectations and headaches. Unfortunately, the meaning and implication of equality are often exaggerated, so much so it has ruined the structure of relationships altogether. Women are more inclined to push for love-equality since they believe in the importance of love in relationships more eagerly.

In fact, relationships' chances of survival have declined drastically with love becoming the main success factor—because love itself cannot survive in relationships. Actually, a cynical interpretation of *love* implies that it flourishes only by deprivation and not through a relationship. Perhaps believing that relationships (marriage) kill(s) love is cynical. However, we can safely say that after the initial stages of companionship, couples encounter a peculiar atmosphere dissimilar to their initial perceptions of *love*. The new atmosphere is shaped according to partners' odd personal needs and personality aspects, which are hardly ever spiritual or logical. Therefore, in light of all these clues, both a more meaningful view of love and a better perspective of relationships are essential. The question is why should not our culture focus on factors that are effective in prolonging relationships without depending on love too much? And the question is why we cannot identify these relevant factors of success for relationships? The answer is that we really do not understand the true nature of love and relationships in the present era. And we have not yet grasped the importance of developing a relationship framework.

Many of us might realize eventually that our perceptions of an ideal relationship are unrealistic and then lower our expectations. We may end up thinking *practical* at the end, but not before hurting ourselves and our partners for a long time with our idealism and misperceptions. Often it would be too late anyway. The meaning of 'practical' mostly emerges in a type of submission, 'a sense of resignation and disappointment,' that eventually prevails in relationships nowadays. Most relationships contain good doses of resignation and disappointment. On the other hand, many people may lose good companionship opportunities due to their unrealistic demands. They destroy their marriages or look for an idol until most of their useful lives are wasted on dreams. Some of them might then further damage their pride, integrity, and convictions when they keep downgrading their expectations drastically for the sake of getting into a relationship quickly despite its obvious flaws and predictable headaches.

People seek love (mostly ELove) to satisfy a large variety of their personal needs. They have some impressions about the meaning of love, and they have a variety of motives that they try to satisfy by their expressions of love. Their main motives are:

- To *communicate* with their partners.
- To express their basic *feelings*.
- To release *psychological* pressures.
- To mimic their *spiritual* needs.
- To *control* their partners.
- To *manipulate (abuse)* their partners.

These motives drive us to use the word 'love' rather sloppily. In the absence of a better word to express our exact motives (or just for hiding them), using the word 'love' for so many purposes has become customary. However, it is important to keep our expectations from exchanging 'love' phrases in proper perspective.

Obviously, the word 'love' covers a large variety of meanings and none of them really reflects true love (SLove). Also, note that love is perceived and applied differently by each individual according to his/her psychological and circumstantial needs. It has no definite meaning to draw upon or set expectations for. We can apply it arbitrarily only to soothe our need for compassion without making an issue out of it or expecting long-term commitment on that basis. "You said you loved me!" is a common complaint when couples interpret love according to their arbitrary and ambiguous perceptions. It is perhaps time now to stop this confusion and couples' futile sufferings in their relationships.

Aside from our selfish need for ELove, we also seek love because we sincerely believe it can bring us that ultimate happiness. We see happiness only in the arms of that special person who fits the image of a perfect soul mate. We hope to complete our existence by finding him/her. This reflects our strong instinctual need for spiritual love (SLove). On the other hand, SLove causes negative feelings, such as jealousy, loneliness, depression, and possessiveness; and there is usually nothing we can do about this demon.

Need for Sex

Sex is a *basic* relationship need as much as it is a *basic* personal need. Therefore, conflicts arise when couples' higher needs (e.g., compassion or ELove) hinder the satisfaction of their instinctual need for sex. Sex has become conditional upon satisfying many higher personal needs of partners, especially love and compassion that partners are normally least capable of delivering. Under this circumstance, the basic sexual need of partners is constantly threatened when some other aspects of their relationship are not perfect, which is usually too often.

Overall, we can say that sex is the most reasonable expectation from relationships. Since couples do not wish to look outside their relationships to fulfil this urge, they must depend on their relationships to satisfy this essential need. In reality, however, partners often withdraw sex as a tool for emotional blackmail or retaliation. In addition, sometimes partners cannot cooperate in this regard and thus look for sex elsewhere. The new social setting has spread this crooked mentality. Meanwhile, sexual freedom feels so urgent to people like a natural need with minimal ethical importance. Nonetheless, nothing can be done about this need beyond what everybody already knows and practices the best way they can. This is just another source of conflict in relationships. All other dramas surrounding sex cannot be helped either. Most of them are psychologically explainable and rather inevitable.

Sex has another instinctual purpose, too, of course. The strong urge to procreate encourages especially women to seek a companion more actively. Men usually play a lesser role in pursuing this heavenly purpose (the reproductive aspect of sex, of course). Therefore, while both genders have huge sexual drives, they have different motives (and biological clocks) for acting upon it. These differences lead to clashes, especially after children are born. Women focus more on the welfare of children and become too possessive of them. Sometimes, it seems absurd the way they try to protect their children even from their husbands. Accordingly, men feel abandoned and neglected sexually and emotionally. They might also face occasional hostility if their interference or means of child rearing does not coincide with their wives'. On the other hand, men are often accused of their shallow pursuit of sex, although women are catching up in this regard too. The need to experiment with our sexuality is now in full force by both genders.

Anyway, nobody can be blamed for the way their sexual instincts dictate their behaviour and priorities in life, or when their lifestyles jeopardize the satisfaction of a basic need like sex. Sex has turned into a potent parameter for partners to play their games and tame each other. These are irreversible facts of life that cause relationship quarrels. However, it is important to acknowledge their impacts and sources instead of denying (or arguing about) them tenaciously. Women's rising share of sexual activities and appetite, plus their progressive mentality, approach, and perceived deprivation about sex are emerging social phenomena that would continue to change relationships' format and widen gender conflicts and quarrels.

Need for Equality

Women's urgent and neglected need for equality has brought about a great deal of mayhem and increased gender differences substantially, too, instead of helping relationship or individuals. The new generations must pay a big price to resolve this matter and maybe reduce the gender gap caused by our drive for equality. For one thing, our need and perception of equality has hindered the urgent need for couples to learn about the principles of teamwork in order to compensate for all the symptoms of gender differences widening in the new era.

In fact, eventually teamwork would be the only means to abolish the need for equality struggles. Nowadays, we try to oversimplify, perhaps even abuse, the interworking of relationships by pushing the concept of equality and assuming that all the problems would be solved automatically. We attempted to solve women's personal problems and reduce the amount of intimidation and control by men. However, we have not solved the problems of relationships. In fact, it appears that relationship conflicts have increased dramatically in society the more this concept of equality has been emphasized and enforced. Even worse, women's frustration has increased due to their unfulfilled expectations. The more they have expected from their relationships, the less they have actually ended up receiving (again judging by divorce rates and increasing family conflicts).

Often, women's expectations for equality appear vague, sounding more like whining, with devastating effect on their relationships. Some women's exaggerated demand for equality sometimes looks more like a quest for superiority. Initially, the equality movement sounded logical for overcoming men's superiority. But now, everything appears to be turning around.

periority. But now, everything appears to be turning around. That is, men feel unequal in a world where women set most standards of equality, which appear one-sided or arbitrary. They often feel intimidated by their partners' ambiguous expectations. Many of them have adopted a passive role in their relationships due to the severity of their spouses' views of equality. The problem is that, nowadays, 'equality bargaining' is infected by partners' Ego.

Equality expectations often arise from partners' urge to control one another. The concept of equality is psychologically absurd anyway. This is because everyone inherently believes that his/her logic is superior to other people's, including his/her criteria for defining equality. We strongly believe that we know about everything better than everybody else regardless of his or her gender. A strong tendency exists in most humans to feel superior to others, not equal, although they might pretend to be fair and humble. In modern societies, almost everybody believes in gender equality, but not intellectual equality. By default, our Ego forces us to feel almost perfect in terms of logic, intelligence, cognition and all the rest of the good stuff. The gender equality issue is resolved for the most part, but the inherent sense of superiority can never be erased from people's minds—due to their innate perception of their intellectual superiority. This is the source of all the inequalities nowadays. They are not gender driven but rather Ego driven for both genders. Gender equality is a hot issue nowadays due to the relationships' rising importance and troubles in society, and because everybody (men and women) feels special and superior and not equal.

Obviously, the solution to reduce the 'equality need' frictions is to develop and propagate the sense of teamwork. Once partners learn to focus on teamwork, their obsession for *equal-*

ity subsides. Instead of depending on equality, or superiority, the success of relationships would be measured only by the smooth operation and outcome of teamwork—not the level of one partner's influence over the other. Equality is, by the way, perceived and measured differently by people according to their subjective criteria and emotional maturity. Thus, instead of wasting so much energy on forcing some kind of imaginary equality in relationships, couples must learn to put all those efforts into defining a practical process of teamwork. Teamwork enables couples to contribute to major decisions and feel active in their relationships. However, it does not deprive partners from doing most tasks independently based on their expertise or merely for creating synergy. Partners should be able to decide independently, instead of doubting their authority or identity all the time. They should not lose their confidence and the control of their lives in fear of retaliation.

Indeed, the strength of teamwork lies on its emphasis on partners' independence and objectivity. Their independent (yet objective) opinions are needed for important decisions of the family. This is more in line with the trend in society to promote individualism. However, it also gives partners a chance to use their unique expertise for the benefit of their relationship without being constantly second-guessed by their partners. In teamwork, partners' roles are clear. This is contrary to the existing approach where partners are confused or depressed about their roles because they are mostly preoccupied by equality games. It is indeed too difficult to understand the equality rules, since we have not yet established the objectives and means of *family equality*. Equality, and measuring it, remains at best ambiguous and arbitrary. It lives only in people's imaginations and it manifests in the form of immature games of resistance and confrontation with no definite purpose or guideline.

The concept of 'equality' has initially emerged out of a sense of desperation, but is now being driven mostly by Ego— the urge for superiority. Teamwork, on the other hand, is Self (goodness) and Model (tactfulness) driven. Therefore, it is not too difficult to decide which approach could have a better chance of success in the long run. Couples' quarrels to exert equality would only reinforce the Egos of both partners, which would only lead to more clashes. Besides, as said before, the concept of equality is psychologically flawed anyway, because our prominent Ego absolutely abhors equality. People are psychologically incapable of handling equality because they feel superior in their deepest level of consciousness.

While men and women have the same rights and acknowledge each other's contributions, they need not share the same tasks and roles to ensure equality. This is an obvious concept, but in reality couples waste a lot of energy nowadays, consciously or subconsciously, on measuring the difficulty of various responsibilities and quarrelling about them

The best test of equality in terms of partners' decision making or sharing household affairs is to see how well those activities and processes fit within the guidelines of teamwork. If they do not fit, they are biased, Ego driven, and futile. Conversely, grasping the guidelines of teamwork and implementing them in relationships would enhance partners' Self and Model at the expense Ego—thus more effective relationships. In all, teamwork guidelines would inherently ensure couples' fairer treatment of each other, which is the objective of equality struggles theoretically. By adhering to some basic guidelines for relationships (and teamwork), partners' rights would be best served in an environment built for coexistence. So the question is, if any standards can be invented what would they look like?

Need for Individualism

In line with our struggles for independence and equality, the notions of individualism and identity have found major implications in relationships, too. In particular, they have caused additional gender differences and major barriers for couples' appreciation of the need for teamwork and synergy. Since we insist so much on proving our identity and individualism, it is important to at least know what it means and maybe learn to acquire those qualities truly. In fact, individualism and being a good person is the best way to improve our relationships and reach gender equality, too. Alas, we do not know how to reach it.

Individualism is the nucleus of 'self,' because it must ensure our survival and progress in society while fighting the evils of social living. Its goal is to strengthen our spirit, integrity, and compassion instead of becoming ruthless or losing our resilience. Individualism portrays the simple and pure characteristics of an evolved person with a transcended soul. His/her integrity and compassion lead him/her to deal with others fairly and avoid wickedness. More importantly, however, individualism reflects the traits of a person in peace with him/herself and the world despite the pervasive societal imperfections and weaknesses.

Defining 'individualism' as a transcended state of being rightly shows our mistrust in the inherent purity of human nature. It reflects our realistic view of human character and its influence on our cultures and lifestyles. It reveals our desperate struggle with humans' natural tendency toward immorality as their basic qualities. On the other hand, our societies hinder the advance of individualism as a common human attribute. Unfortunately, individualism and integrity often sound like some rare virtues found only in saints and highly evolved individuals—like divine manifestations beyond most humans' capacity.

Humans' low integrity affects them mostly in their relationships, but also personally. One becomes what he practices as part of coping with all the hypocrisies and deceit in society. Our present social setting forces us to become cruel like everybody else despite our potentials to be a better human being. We see people who have become so absorbed in their evilness that malice has become their real nature. They cannot do anything without some form of treachery even when it does not have a direct benefit to them. Their individuality has simply collapsed to a mere deceit-brain. Strangely enough, they actually fall for their own lies with such deep commitment they often sacrifice even their valuable assets in the process, including their families and friends. The world of deceit and hypocrisy that they choose to live in contradict even the raw social ethics, let alone a sense of humanness. They just float within a vastly crooked illusion of life and behave like the devil.

The Webster's dictionary defines individualism as, 'The conception that all values, rights, and duties originate in individuals.' Thus, individualism seems like an attempt to gain our independence and establish identity, not merely in society, but mostly in our own heads. We like to 'know (about) ourselves' and the possibility of being a better person. Therefore, we strive to assess ourselves in terms of values, rights, and duties that we have adopted (created) in the process of earning and proving our identity.

We try to understand where our values come from, how authentic they are, and how they help humanity and us. In terms of our rights, we ensure they coincide with the rights of others, so that all individuals and society as a whole can move toward a peaceful harmony and relative relief from life hardships. The problem nowadays is that a person's rights often turn into self-serving demands on others for personal gains and interests. People have difficulty making this distinction when looking for their rights. They try to impose their misperceived rights on others deliberately or inadvertently by their egotistical attitude and unrelenting struggle for power and authority with little regard for the rights of other human beings.

With respect to our duties, individualism reiterates our personal obligations and social responsibilities. Some of them are instinctual, such as our duties toward our children and parents. Other duties, e.g., toward our spouses and friends, are expected to come natural to us, too, if genuine feelings exist. However, in reality, people are too self-absorbed nowadays to maintain their integrity and fulfil these types of duties naturally. Therefore, they must extend extra efforts more consciously to discharge their duties to some degree at least. Finally, some duties are mostly moral obligations, such as our duties at work and society. Our passivity in acknowledging and discharging our duties may be intentional or due to mere ignorance. Intentional passivity is hard to repair, as it mostly reflects our pomposity, deep psychological flaws, and the impact of social adaptation. Ignorance, on the other hand, can be remedied a bit easier through self-awareness and involvement.

Overall, individualism reflects the quality of our choices, decisions, and actions, as we determine and practice our rights, values, and duties for accomplishing notable purposes. While the objective of 'individualism' is to strengthen the inherent value of 'self' as a wise and humble person, it also stresses on personal integrity to adjust our values, rights, and duties in line with the needs of all humanity. Individualism is not merely an inner growth and satisfaction, but also an outer reflection of integrity and morality. The Webster's definition of 'individualism' does not quite reflect the need for the rightness of one's values, rights, duties. Yet, without integrity and compassion, we cannot set the right 'values,' as we cannot see their rightness. And we cannot comprehend the value of people's 'rights,' because our criteria of rightness is personal and selfish. Contrary to common view to interpret individualism as a means of self-absorption, its value lies mostly in humility and a person's regard for other individuals' rights. In fact, individualism is an inner exploration instead of an outwardly ostentatious presentation of one's Ego, as it is mostly implied in our common pretensions of individualism.

Individualism evolves only through compassion and modesty while a person gauges the truthfulness of his connection to other individuals, things, and concepts with a genuine interest and care. Only then, s/he can see the rights of other individuals and the values of things and concepts in their purest sense in line with his/her own authentic life purposes. Without compassion and integrity, one lacks the sensitivity and sensibility required for perceiving things or people outside one's rigid and biased prejudgments. The lack of compassion and modesty reflects Ego domination, which is the main hindrance for knowing our 'self.'

Trying to teach people 'individualism' without including all the above noted basic requirements in our definition has been the cause of the present misperceptions about this divine notion. The result of our superficial understanding of individualism has been disastrous because people interpret this

concept as a means of becoming more haughty and demanding instead of learning humility. It has caused more gender
differences and relationship conundrums for people who have
no capacity to go beyond the superficialities of our society.

As one of the seven dimensions of 'self,' individualism is a
source of energy, too. The energy stems from the integrity of
our choices, decisions, and actions. A sense of 'self' realiza-
tion lifts our spirit when we finally choose a modest option
after contemplating many self-serving possibilities, make a
compassionate decision, or take a worthy action. We strive to
make the right choices with integrity and compassion for the
betterment of humanity and for building our own spirit, despite our sour experiences and the normal distractions of social
living. Perfecting every dimension of 'self' brings more energy and wisdom for living peacefully with contentment. This
proactive mentality helps us build our integrity and spirit to go
through life with minimal confusion and distress.

This mentality may help us understand that, contrary to our
immature perception, individualism has nothing to do with
self-centredness and egoism. Rather, it is only the means of
reaching our Self and a sense of selflessness.

Need for Fairness

Equality, independence, and similar self-defining objectives in
the new era are for getting a sense of fairness and justice. We
firmly believe that life owes us the best of everything. We are
convinced that we not only have huge potentialities to offer to
society, but also deserve substantial rewards for what we do
and who we are. We strive to demonstrate our potentialities so
that people can discover and respect us. We change jobs, in-

vent things and ideas, and pursue all sorts of business ventures in order to prove ourselves.

However, many forces prevent our dreams from coming true. Most of us realize gradually that our potentialities would never be recognized or rewarded, and thus we attribute this atrocity to the world's unfairness. It feels as though people deliberately refuse to acknowledge us for what we can do, think, and feel—our unique potentialities. They refuse to provide honest feedback, encouragement, respect, or compensation, which we seriously believe we deserve. Thus, we get frustrated and convinced that both life and people are unfair.

We often feel this way. Actually, our frustrations about life's unfairness and people's malice are warranted often too. The fact is that while everybody is self-centred and mostly concerned about his/her our own needs, desires, and Ego, fairness becomes an illusion automatically. We are not unfair necessarily out of spite, but mainly because we are self-serving individuals and must be fairer and nicer to ourselves first. We need the most and best of everything for ourselves and those whose friendship and loyalty we need. If any charity is still left in us to share, only then we might be less prejudiced occasionally. These are real facts and we must recognize that we cannot do anything about the matter. The rule is that we do not have enough compassion toward others, especially strangers—the primitive law of survival and success!

Another point is that we are often personally responsible for stirring the feelings of unfairness by exaggerating our needs and potentialities and setting unreasonable expectations. It is in fact a sign of our unreasonableness (unfairness) when we expect people to appreciate 'who we are' while we persistently overstate our capabilities and remain arrogant. Even if we were honest with our presentation of who we are, still it is not usually possible for others to appreciate who we are. Thus, ultimately, either our perceived unfairness or actual social prejudices cause us stress and confusion. Yet, we must somehow learn to come to terms with this *unfairness* too.

'Feeling unfairness and inducing it ourselves' is a human shortfall. This awareness provides a basic consolation, as we can blame humans' nature for feeling and acting this way. Yet, some people can deal with unfairness better. They disallow the feeling of self-pity or aggression overwhelm them when they face unfairness. While they do not measure their potentialities and self-worth in terms of external rewards and recognition, the feeling of unfairness occurs to them less frequently too. In addition, when a person develops his/her inner confidence and actualizes his/her potentialities, the question of unfairness hardly surfaces.

We have two choices on this matter. One option is to accept unfairness as an irreversible reality, like so many other limitations of social living. This mentality is hard to adopt, but it can save us a lot of agony and energy. More importantly, this mentality can save our relationships, too. The other more prevalent option is to let self-pity aggravate our stress and aggression toward others. Taking fairness less seriously helps us make better choices in life, however. Instead of self-pity or aggression, we could contemplate the chance of creating a life of needlessness or independence, while we dream about the possibility of humans becoming less self-serving and selfish eventually.

Indeed, we deserve to be understood and appreciated, but it is somewhat unreasonable to expect others to care enough, or be able, to perceive our feelings and thoughts accurately. People have too many problems and personal agendas to care about the depth of other people's personality, potentialities,

and thoughts. Their judgments are at best hasty if not mali-
cious. This is the rule and sentiments of the perceived world.
This is human nature, because we have not built our spirits,
especially the spirit of fairness. We must accept the reality of
unfairness, despite the pervasive discriminations and prejudices at work and family life. As another step for exploring
our divine potentialities, we must adjust our perspective of
unfairness and our expectations from people in this regard.

Need for Control

It is quite bizarre that we are so obsessed about fairness, equality, independence, and all the other needs discussed in this
chapter, but still are so eager to control others. We have a
strong urge to control our surroundings to maintain order in
our lives. We wish to minimize unexpected threats by foresee-
ing events or obstacles. The more complex our societies and
interactions become, the more we feel a need to control the
sources of potential threats to our physical and mental welfare.
This is particularly true because nowadays we trust people
much less than we did a few decades ago. We know that
crooks are everywhere, trying to take advantage of our na-
ïveté. Accordingly, our defence mechanisms and need for control are further developed to survive in this environment. Even
banks, stock brokers, mortgage brokers, and other supposedly
government-controlled entities regularly lure us into bad decisions and losing our life savings. Hardly do governments step
in to support citizens because capitalism gives a higher priority to free enterprise than individuals. Therefore, we feel the
pressure to control our lives better and make sure we are not
victimized. When we get into relationships, the need for control feels even more urgent and necessary. We have to protect

our families and ourselves. However, we must also be careful about our families' intentions and possible hidden agendas. Unfortunately, the more society advances, the less it appears that we can trust our partners in relationships. Therefore, we try to control them in order to minimize the possibility of getting hurt by them. However, we also wish to control them with the assumption that this would be the best way to protect and prolong our relationships. Naturally, the result of all this controlling is that couples hate, and stress out, each other. Couples' need for independence is challenged when partners try to control each other in hopes of making their relationship last longer. Need for control is a major cause of gender quarrels.

As noted, it is just weird that we do not appreciate the contradictions that our needs for control and independence cause throughout the society, especially in our relationships.

Even love is often abused to satisfy one's need for control. One reason for 'love' being in such demand, nowadays, is that a person can supposedly control his/her partner better if that partner is in love with him/her. We yearn for SLove to fulfil our need for self-gratification and spirituality. However, in reality, nowadays, we mostly end up seeking ELove for compassion and/or controlling our partners. We crave love, even though we are often not capable of giving love in return. We want to be loved for several reasons mentioned in this book, but also for controlling our partner through love dependency.

A lot of personal spirit and potentialities are dampened in relationships due to partners' urge to control each other, sometimes even through (real or fake) love. Both partners lose the opportunity for full growth and self-actualization when even one partner is a control freak.

Need for Domination

Our need for control often gets out of hand and soon we like to manipulate and dominate one another, especially in our relationships. The evil of domination and exploitation is an encompassing human trait and has become an epidemic in society. In marital relationships, in particular, the need for domination becomes intense due to the high level of emotions involved and the proximity of couples' activities and decision-making processes. It is weird when couples (especially women) insist on equality, but seem capable of implementing this presumed sense of equality only through domination. As two main contributing factors, egoism and need for domination cause almost all marital conflicts. When we communicate with one another, we set out automatically to dominate (or manipulate) the situation and our partner by insisting on our point and position to win in our dialogues. When we attempt to change our partner, again it is the sign of our inner urges to dominate and turn him/her to a personality that we are most comfortable with. Thus, we look for excuses to blame and nag, mostly because we do not feel to have enough domination. It also shows that we do not wish to curb our urges and intentions of dominating the family structure and our spouse. Blaming and nagging are largely personal tactics to wear down our partner and take over the situation and decisions.

Of course, signs of teamwork and cooperation emerge from time to time mostly through Model. However, soon enough, our Ego takes over and proceeds to dominate the situation and our partner. Of course, we all try to hide our urges for domination and manipulation, especially before marriage when we use Model to manoeuvre and soften the person we like. Then our urge for domination and manipulation eventually erupt with full force.

Our urges for domination of family life and our partner obviously reflect our intention to control the decisions, actions and behaviours of all family members. We need to do this in order to ensure things occur in the ways we think is best for all. Supposedly, we have the good intention of saving the relationship from going the wrong way, but also controlling our destiny and independence as much as possible. When our needs for control and independence are threatened by the objections and interferences of our spouse, we quickly see the need to dominate the situation and our spouse. We do not want surprises, risks, and troubles. We like everything to proceed smoothly as we have planned personally and perhaps with input from our parents or friends. We simply feel a need to control family issues and situations. However, when we find out that our spouse likes to influence those same issues and situations, we are left with no option but to control our partner as well. Thus, the logical tactic in our minds is to control any situation and person that may affect the outcome of our plans and expectations for a kind of life and relationship we prefer. We expect our partner to understand and agree with our values, perceptions of life, and logic. We believe our way of life is the most logical one and thus everybody should agree with it after we explain it to them, in our often crooked language. However, if we cannot come to some agreement, we plan and persist to remain in control somehow, or else we get agitated and retaliatory all the time.

Our urge for domination also emerges from our desires to possess our partner like a personal property. Possessiveness by itself is a psychological defect that most of us are inflicted with at some degree. Possessiveness induces our need for control and domination not only over the physical aspects of our partner's life, like what s/he does, where s/he goes, or what she wears, but also on his/her thoughts. We want our partner think in certain ways for our convenience, but also because we want to be in control and possess him/her mind too.

Our urges for domination and possessiveness not only hurt our partner and relationship, but also annihilate our individuality and peace. Our jealousies, retaliations, nagging and blaming, and all other negative psychological reactions, result from domination and possessiveness. The amount of time and energy we waste to deal with, or confront, the causes of our jealousy, retaliation and the rest of it, are quite substantial. Our useless jealousy and possessiveness cripple our brain and deprive us from pursuing rewarding and relaxing activities. We grasp this fact in the latter stages of our lives when the futility of our jealousies and retaliations become clear.

Instead of drowning ourselves deep in a state of helplessness by our need for love, which quickly raises our urges for possessiveness and domination, we can concentrate on our essential personal needs. We can pay attention to the joint needs of partners (especially for independence and equality) in modern marriages.

Tactics for Satisfying Our Needs

Our needs for control and domination are in fact our tactics for satisfying all the other needs that were discussed in this chapter. Blaming, nagging, getting emotional, and retaliation are some other tactics we use for satisfying our needs. Therefore, a few of these tactics are explained briefly here.

Retaliation and Nagging

We imagine that retaliation makes our partners suffer and thus perhaps change their attitudes. However, our retaliations cause more resistance and counter-retaliations that only ruin the foundation of relationships. We blame others and nag regularly in order to control, manipulate, or dominate others. Nagging and blaming also help us relieve ourselves from life frustrations and agonies. Therefore, we grow a crooked habit to look outward to blame something or somebody instead of looking inside ourselves and detect not only the real sources of our stress, but also how defective we are personally.

If partners trust and respect each other and have good communication skills, they can exchange compassion and sympathy, share their problems, and rid themselves of life tensions and stress. However, without trust and respect, partners feel spiteful toward each other. Their ideas and suggestions usually erupt in hostile tones and their marriage turns into the battleground for firing blames and nagging at each other. Having a marriage partner appears to be the most convenient way to relieve our tensions by nagging at him/her. However, the outcome could be quite devastating when partners get carried away unconsciously over time.

Partners share many responsibilities. They make joint decisions and take actions that affect all family members. Not only they blame each other for the ways joint decisions turn out, but also for things that neither partner has been directly involved with or intended to do. They find a way to attribute a failure or problem to their partner sometimes unconsciously and sometimes in retaliation for something else s/he has done to them before. Sometimes, they are miserable because of their per-

sonal problems or failures and then find a convenient occasion
to blame it on their partners somehow indirectly and generally.
They may even arrive at general personal conclusions to
blame their partner, for example by making comments like, "I
have lost all my confidence because of the way you have
treated me!", or "I have become old because of you!", etc.
Very often one partner is suffering from his/her incomplete
and boring life and then finds all sorts of reasons to nag at his/
her partner and blame him/her routinely even when there is no
specific issue to bug him/her with.

The irony is that if by a miracle we could be unmarried
again, most likely we would be as much, and perhaps even
more, miserable and full of failures, and nobody would be
around to blame it on or nag to. It is our own self-inflicted
misery that we condemn our partner for so relentlessly and
irresponsibly. And usually we feel, express, and expect love at
the same time! In fact, we still expect to be *spoiled* when we
keep blaming him/her and nagging all the time!—often for not
being spoiled enough!

Often one partner has no self-fulfilling activities to keep
him/herself amused and happy, and then keeps blaming his/
her partner for not finding interesting and entertaining things
to do together and not giving this matter enough thought and
time. The blamed partner may believe s/he is doing a lot already, and is willing to participate in other joint activities
whenever possible too, but also has some personal interests
that the blaming partner does not care for. Personal interests of
one partner become the source of envy for the other partner
and an excuse to nag constantly. S/he just hopes that, by nagging and blaming, the other partner would eventually give up
his/her personal interests, which seem to be drawing all his/her
attention (love) and thus a perceived conflict. Sometimes, it

appears that the whole point of our nagging is merely to wear our partner out and make him/her as miserable as we are. We hate his/her relative peace.

A conflict arises when one or both partners cannot separate their personal needs from relationship (joint) needs, and thus set their expectations erroneously. Or, when one partner attempts to follow his personal needs (as simple as listening to music or watching sports), which threatens the mental security of the other partner, as s/he feels neglected. One partner may prefer to do almost everything together whereas the other has less patience for so many aspects of his/her partner's activities, or prefers to do some activities alone. This shows that they have not discussed and agreed upon a workable relationship model suitable for them.

Partners' blaming and nagging attitude may be either a deliberate or an unconscious reaction, but either way, they exhaust partners and their relationship. Ego drives this attitude with no sign of Model's flexibility to soothe even the elementary frictions that erupt in all relationship. Naturally, Self is obviously absent when nagging and blaming goes on. Ordinarily, using Model can help in expressing one's sufferings and needs in a more passionate and convincing manner, hoping at least for some tangible and productive communication and perhaps some sympathy. However, with nagging and blaming, we lose the chance of showing our honest feelings, mainly through Model or Self, to keep the situation under control. In general, blaming and nagging reflect our inner sufferings due to our unrelenting need for attention.

With blaming and nagging, we actually put our partner on notice to prepare for a battle. We merely agitate the relationship without concern or conscience about causing conflict and confrontation. Both the nagger and naggee recognize this and put up their defences. The nagging partner is most likely empty of Model, at least temporarily, and is forcefully attacking with a boosted Ego. Therefore, the other partner is left with the options of surrendering and leaving the battlefield, igniting the battle, or attempting to initiate a peace negotiation. If s/he uses the latter option, which is in most cases the wisest one, s/he draws upon his/her Model to bring his/her partner and situation under control. 'Model' is capable of making peace offerings in a nice package and this is one of those times when Model can really prove its value. We can use Model to invoke the softer emotions of our partner if we know how and if possible at all. Once we normalize the situation somewhat with compassion and perhaps some help from our Self, we can reduce Model and concentrate on peace terms and means of maintaining it in the long run. We should not expect things to work out permanently with one or even dozen negotiations, because nagging is a deep symptom and habit that partners do not give up easily. However, our patient effort for peace is the only chance left before we lose our total confidence in our partner and marriage.

In addition, we should find the courage and patience to distinguish constructive criticism—as part of teamwork—from blaming and nagging. Some couples have difficulty in expressing their intentions properly. A constructive criticism by one partner may be received as a blatant blame and nagging if it is expressed in a wrong tone of voice. As a result, partners get into needless arguments and quarrels, instead of benefiting from each other's wisdom and insight. Drawing the line between blame and objective criticism may become a blur when expressed improperly or when the recipient is psychologically resistant to any type of consultation process. Nevertheless, both partners must realize one fact sooner or later: Blaming does not help or solve any problem, and thus it does not matter how forcefully we condemn our partner or a situation. In the final analysis, it does not matter whose fault it is that a couple cannot communicate and resolve their problems. Pointing fingers of blame to each other only damages their relationship further. Partners should instead define and agree on real problems and causes of frictions regardless of whose fault they are.

We should stop taking marriage problems personal, even if we believe one partner is probably more in fault than the other. Instead, only concentrating on objective thinking, goodwill, and solutions may resolve marital problems, and it can happen only through calm negotiations, not personalizing the issues and blaming each other.

From our personal experiences or by referring to the lists of gender qualities and symptoms in Part I, many of us can draw a general conclusion about the possibility of one gender having a higher tendency for nagging, blaming, manipulation, and retaliation. Definite proofs are not available to the author about this matter today. Yet, it seems rather likely that women do it more often due to their decisiveness facing men's passivity and procrastination, their overall authority in the family being challenged by men, and their deep frustration with men. This topic will be addressed in a future book in this series.

Logic and Emotions

We use both our logic and emotions as potent tactics to satisfy all our personal needs noted above. Yet, at the end, our logic seems to fail and our emotions drain during all the relationship quarrels we get into for satisfying our seemingly legitimate needs. A main hurdle in relationships is that gender differences and conflicts arise from the simple fact that women like to deal with relationship issues more emotionally and intuitively, while men try to use their demented sense of logic, which has already made them dogmatic anyway. In that sense, both human intuition and logic are incapable of helping us. Therefore, it seems that only through self-awareness and use of a relationship framework we might bring some objectivity back into relationships.

Our intuition is useful for some aspects of our lives, especially finding our sense of spirituality and Self. However, intuition cannot help us with our daily lives, especially relationships, in such a complex social setting. The same thing can be said about the impotency of human logic. It rarely helps us, mostly because we do not have a real sense of logic and fairness for making our judgments.

In the final analysis, unfortunately, we must agree that human logic and intuition would never be able to explain so many phenomena and questions about the universe, Creation, humanity, our relationships, etc. Yet, we do not wish to acknowledge our ignorance and use this awareness to at least stop judging everything and everyone so adamantly. We do not wish to admit our mistakes, not even in those cases where our crooked actions and selfish beliefs are unexplainable even by human logic, intuition, science, or plausible theories.

Self-sabotage

As a great example about the impotency of our logic and intuition, we can study the way we usually go about choosing our partners and how some forces of evil always seem to interfere. A great majority of us gets entangled in this condition due to many emotional as well as personal needs and insecurities that overwhelm us on such occasions. Our logic and intuition lose even their basic values and we choose someone with whom we have the least level of compatibility.

Obviously, partners' compatibility partially improves their chances of communicating and relating to one another. Objectivity is introduced in their relationships at many levels when they share certain values and have compatible mentalities. In reality, however, even this basic tool for introducing objectivity is constantly sabotaged by partners. That is, not only we do not know how to measure compatibility, but also ignore the signs of incompatibility when they are clearly in front of us. For example, when we are in love or need a companion urgently, we ignore all the potential hassles of incompatibility. It seems as if some evil forces are at work to make us choose the wrong partners for ourselves. Sometimes, we go out of our ways to ignore compatible partners in favour of incompatible ones. Sometimes, we prefer jerks because they seem to challenge us. Many reasons exist for this behaviour. They all relate to the effects of inner forces and outer forces that make us jump into relationships prematurely. The initial chemistry that partners feel toward each other often obscures their objectivity. In addition, quite often, we do not get the opportunity to be choosy. When someone shows compassion and love, we stop worrying about the consequences of gross incompatibility. This is true, especially, since the hassles of relationships are not felt until we get involved in one. Or, we often believe that the next partner and the next relationship would be different, i.e., it would be manageable and nice!

Unfortunately, the value of compatibility tests is low at the present time anyway. However, our persistence and preference to ignore any clue or perception of incompatibility shows the low value of our logic and dangers of intuition nowadays. Still, most couples prefer to depend mostly on their intuition, chemistry, and arbitrary values that society and parents have injected into their minds about relationships' success factors. Sometime in the far future, people may finally find access to reliable compatibility tests to understand where they stand and what kind of a relationship they might be able to build together. Meanwhile, even basic compatibility tests and relationship can help couples to pinpoint at least their incompatibilities and potential problem areas.

In a group therapy session, a dozen divorced men and women were asked to mention the main reason for choosing their ex-spouses. The answers were quite informative. The typical answers were as follows:

- Mother/father figure
- Out of pity, I felt sorry for her/him
- Lifestyle change
- To stabilize my life
- To have a home
- I loved him/her (the most popular answer)

Obviously, when the initial purpose of a relationship is not valid or solid, the chances of bringing objectivity into it would be slim. After a while, couples realize their mistakes and begin to resent their partners and themselves for being dragged into a doomed relationship incapable of satisfying their needs (which are superficial most often anyway). Some other reasons for couples choosing the wrong partners are: physical attraction, lust, age, biological clock, social/family pressure, psychological dysfunction, misperceptions, ELove, obsessions, material issues, insecurity, lack of meaningful criteria to use, loneliness.

Based on limited (unscientific) findings, the author has developed a cynical hypothesis that explains so many of relationship problems. That is, the author believes that people usually feel chemistry toward individuals whom they are not compatible with in any justifiable measure. The hypothesis stipulates the opposite as well: Compatible individuals normally feel little or no chemistry toward one another. Still the latter group has a better chance of building and managing a good relationship for themselves compared with the first group, i.e., incompatible lovers. If these theories hold water, the question is, 'Why Nature make couples choose wrong partners for themselves?'

CHAPTER NINE
Gender Roles

THE discussions in this book show many bizarre trends emerging in relationships, which are also widening gender differences. A major cause of this deteriorating situation is the way genders interpret new social values and their means of relating. In fact, they no longer know their gender roles that could match any logical type of relationship principles. Many dilemmas and quarrels overwhelm marital lives nowadays as couples struggle to cope with the new relationship environment while asserting their dignity and individualism as well. They like to deal with their needs for both dependence and independence. Some couples seek separation with the minimal inconvenience in their relationships (high need for independence and individualism); and some couples accept abuse and adultery as they are too apprehensive about loneliness and isolation (high need for dependence and compassion).

A main force affecting relationships adversely without anyone's fault is that women are in a state of transition in terms of the progressive role they like to play in society and relationships. The transition period mainly refers to the process of men and women developing their workable identities and learning their relationship roles in the new era. However, in reality, it refers to the long period for couples, especially women, to realize that their expectations from relationships are not logical and feasible.

The social changes and the women's new role are obviously necessary. However, the process is not still complete, and, even worse, it has not been smooth from the start. The means and the format of women's new role are not grasped even by the majority of women, let alone by men who are expected to not only know what the new format should be, but also respond positively too. Nobody seems to know, let alone agree, where the boundaries must be in order to facilitate this transition without now putting men under undue pressure. Women wish to be assertive and express their personal needs freely. However, implementing or enforcing this new role smoothly has not been successful yet, simply because of the human inner forces that are still ruling people's personalities and hindering their communication.

Women's transition from submissiveness to assertiveness surely requires a long period of trials and errors to reach a workable steady state. However, the present generation has no time and patience to let the genders' historical predispositions get adjusted smoothly. And to make the matter worse, the old wounds have not still had a chance to heal. Thus, a special situation has emerged: Women find it necessary to become aggressive in order to attain the assertiveness they need urgently. Especially for some women, who do not quite understand the meaning and mode of practicing assertiveness, the only practical approach appears to be retaliation and by resorting to aggression to make their points clear. For men, the new demands are not only threatening their identities, but also confusing them (again considering the power of inner forces ruling their minds). Women's expectation from men—to over-

come the psychological forces that shape their (men's) identity—is unrealistic. They are ignoring the fact that men cannot
readily revamp all those inner forces built within them. Making the required changes is an extremely difficult task, even in
a timelier manner, even if men agreed with the changes
women are expecting of them. However, women cannot wait
for history to take its course. They cannot struggle forever to
prove their viewpoints rationally to stubborn men. So, they
must put their feet down to get things done; what other option
do they have? They live only one short life. They cannot wait
for decades and centuries for men to gradually understand and
acknowledge the validity of the new roles for both men and
women. Women are tired of waiting for a miracle to clarify
the new gender roles in relationships. They must take this crucial matter in their own hands. Alas, the problem is that neither gender knows what their roles and identities should be.

Within this confusing situation, both genders' destructive
aggressions are complicating the transition process. Instead of
progress, we witness sabotages and retaliation, more games,
more divorces, more passivity, and family murder suicides.
The bottom line is that men have lost their identities (whatever
it was, good or bad) and do not understand the sensibility of
what is expected of them. Women are frustrated, too, because
they cannot enforce a new identity, which they believe they
know what it is—an identity they believe they deserve. To
women, it appears that men are resisting or careless at best.
Therefore, everybody is drowning in despair during this transition process. We can only hope that we eventually emerge out
of this chaotic situation with a new workable identity. It might
be a wishful thinking, though, when nobody even knows what
these identities should look like. We do not even know how
the transition process may evolve without too much agony and

more divorces. We have not even clarified the genders' needs
and demands, or the format of their interactions in that supposedly innovative setting. The only clear fact is that change,
if possible at all, cannot happen overnight, especially when no
one knows how this transition and the affirmation of the new
roles should happen. The result of the current confusion is that
partners finally get fed up with their struggles to convince
each other about their self-conceived new roles and imaginary
relationship rules. Accordingly, men and women mistrust the
opposite gender much more than their own.

Therefore, partners try to dominate one another or resort to
divorce. Some may just give up and play only a passive role.
Meanwhile, most couples feel trapped and their relationships
remain in limbo; a bunch of men and women without clear
identities, put under relentless pressure by both inner and outer
forces. Under the hostile environment of relationships, we
have actually turned into another destructive *outer force* for
our partners. And we are facing a global identity crisis too.
With no clear gender identities in our modern societies, we
have been importing our vague values to less modernized nations as well!

Like most creatures, we humans instinctually prefer our
autonomy and sense of adventure, especially sexuality. Let us
stop pretending otherwise. Our Egos (and the urge for independence) prevent us from being dependable instinctually.
The discussions in this book provide a reasonable picture of
the way gender differences in fact goad men and women to
resist (or even fight off) each other. Of course, this does not
mean that they do not fall in love or try to support each other.
However, many of these compassionate gestures are tentative
or the residues of old cultural norms and religions. Nowadays,

humans have to make special efforts to get along and share their lives, especially the opposite sexes.

An obvious clue that humans are not instinctually programmed to live together permanently, without some form of binding principles, is their amazing craving for sexual freedom. The urge to experience sex with many partners is in almost all human beings. We put too much emphasis on sex with different partners, somewhat instinctually and partly as a means of finding happiness.

A cute *relationship* instinct is that men usually try to avoid commitment while women want to lure them into it. Is this a symptom of the women's instinctual need for procreation? Probably not, because women and men of all ages have these urges. Are men's avoidance and women's temptation, thus, only a 'condition' developed as a result of people's marital experiences throughout the history of mankind? It is hard to say, except for the fact that women seek dependency more naturally, especially during maternity. Overall, this condition (both genders' resistance toward commitment) will most likely become even more prevalent in the future as men find it more difficult every day to respond to women's newer needs and demands and women find men less and less tolerable. With mistrust rising so fast, the future of relationships seems doomed.

We have accepted the theory of evolution that connects humans to primates and other creatures in general. In the great kingdom of God, the primary role of the male and the female is to reproduce (sexual urge). Their secondary role is to protect one another against adversaries and harsh environments. In particular, the role of the female in protecting and upbringing their offspring is quite prominent. Males are usually less attached to the offspring, and even toward the female, once the initial mating process is complete. Often the female plays a major role in cooling off the relationship too, especially after the offspring gets strong. The male obeys by keeping its distance or moving away altogether. Humans are seemingly driven by similar instincts, despite the social norms devised to keep them focused and tactful. The evidence for similar instincts in humans is not hard to find. We know that:

- Women are more eager to procreate. Their biological clock goads them to get this matter resolved as soon as possible. Women also have a higher urge for parenthood. Thus, they are more anxious to find a suitable man and lure him in for the ultimate objective of creating children. Although the women's inherent need for reproduction seems to compete with their career ambitions nowadays, this condition is mostly superficial, as explained below. Deep down, they are more attached to, and protective of, their children than men are. Actually, their need for reproduction is often more important to them than their urge for independence or career, unlike men. Meanwhile, women's higher urge and urgency for procreation stir their higher need for dependency on men during maternity at least.

- Women show less interest in their husbands when children begin to satiate their emotional needs. Often, children become more important to them than their husbands have ever been. Accordingly, their urge and courage for independence grow when the main objective of nature (reproduction) is fulfilled. Of course, if husbands happen to lose their interest or their focus during this confusing process (game), women eventually look for another mate to satisfy their inherent dependency needs and passion.

- Both genders, but particularly men, are lured by other people's charm once their initial attraction to their spouses wears off. Especially when people age, they crave the company of younger people. They feel vibrant and young when they get the attention of the opposite sex and often believe they can revive their youth by pursuing new adventures, instead of continuing the same life routines with an old, nagging spouse. All of us have this weakness—perhaps a natural way of responding to our psychological need for adventure. The fact that some people do not act upon this natural feeling, due to their sense of ethics, fear, or their integrity, does not change the basic principle about people's natural urge to experience love and sex with someone else other than their spouses. If we get the opportunity, only seldom we might resist the temptation.

- People resent monotony and get depressed if new adventures are not instilled in their lives rather regularly. Living with the same partner often becomes too monotonous.
- The evidence about human hormones indicates that we are not content to live with a partner and in fact have an urge to satisfy a variety of our emotional needs with several partners.

Therefore, people are not mentally (or instinctually) built to tolerate monogamy for many years, especially in a society like ours, which gives so much value to pleasure and making the best use of our lives.

Repercussions of Gender Differences

The repercussions of the rising gender alienation due to all the points made in this book need deeper scrutiny by both individuals and governments. The rising level of relationship conundrums would affect society drastically in the coming years in at least four ways:

Marital Relationships: The state of marital relationships would continue to deteriorate when couples feel more alienated and do not understand the roles they should play as a wife or husband. More relationships would also fail when couples do not grasp their gender identities and cannot find means of relating effectively and without too much friction.

Personal Turmoil: As we fail to manage our relationships, cannot find a good companion, or face the hassles of separation and raising our children alone, our mental and physical health is threatened significantly.

Children's Mindsets: Family alienation due to gender differences and incoherent gender identities has weakened not only family values, but also couples' abilities to teach the right stuff of life to their children. Instead, they are spoiled and misled in terms of life's objectives and capacities.

Next Generations: As alienation and gender differences increase, and while children are not getting the right education about life, every generation would face more turmoil, self-alienation, relationship failures, and depression.

Epilogue

IF couples were not so adamant (needy) about controlling their partners, and if people stopped encouraging one another to look for a perfect relationship and love, they could enjoy many important benefits of relationships. Alas, our obsession for love, happiness, objects, power, and domination is hindering the possibility of enjoying our relationships. Both genders are responsible for some aspects of these shortfalls in some ways.

Gender differences have become more obvious and prevalent in the new era and they will continue to be responsible for a good portion of relationship conflicts. In fact, partners' struggles to establish their gender identities and balance their needs for dependence and independence would lead to further alienation in relationships and partners' rising inner conflicts and frustration. In addition to gender differences and genders' search for their identities, the present social setting and many other relationship and personal quirks (as discussed in this book) also make it difficult for partners to relate to each other. This vast scope of potential problems has made relationship environments too complex and unmanageable. We get more confused about the objectives of relationships every day and feel more frustrated and helpless to relate emotionally, effectively, and efficiently. All these deteriorating trends will continue to get more out of control in the future decades, unless couples change their mentalities about the purposes and potentials of relationships and realign their expectations accordingly. It is also very important for scholars and governments to find some solutions urgently and revamp the existing laws that are in fact contributing to the deterioration of relationship environment.

As a major step, people and society must realize and work on the five fundamental facts about gender qualities and quirks mentioned near the beginning of this book (page 14) and repeated below due to its importance:

1. Although genders' high qualities and symptoms irritate the opposite gender, without such disparity they would have tortured each other and ruined their relationships even more. Just imagine both genders being equally decisive and active based on their intuitions, or were both passive. Not only more frictions would have erupted all the time between partners, but also their whole life outcome would have become even more risky without at least some basic checks and balances that the present gender differences impose on relationships.

2. People have much more common traits and quirks than they have differences. Genders have many common personality attributes, such as ambition, greed, and a big host of crooked personal needs like the ones discussed in Chapter Eight. The amount of relationship frictions caused by those common needs and traits of people, regardless of their gender, is probably as much as it is caused by gender differences.

3. Each gender quality and its symptoms are related to the other personality attributes (qualities and symptoms) for that gender. For example, men's passivity is the outcome of their cautious mind, loose nature, realism, poor identity, etc. Therefore, people cannot change their personality attributes readily even if they agreed they were destructive for them or their relationships.

4. The challenge for couples is to learn to somehow apply their conflicting gender qualities to their advantage in order to relate more effectively and create synergy in their relationships. This objective should eventually feel natural and logical to them. Then they can find means of doing it through compromise and teamwork by respecting their conflicting qualities wisely instead of remaining self-centred and dogmatic about their gender identities and whimsical ideals.

5. Accordingly, the first step to move toward this sacred objective is for people and society to revamp their mentalities about the purposes and potentials of relationships and become rather realistic for reaching a more practical end.

References

List of References

The following main concepts and terms used in this book are explained further or quoted in this section merely for scholars' review and interested readers' ease of reference.

1. Love definitions
2. Definitions of Four Personality Factors
3. Personality Chart and Ratings
4. Other Uses of the Personality Chart
5. Personality Factors, Gender Qualities and Symptoms
6. Sample Personality Ratings

Love Definitions

Three types of love are mentioned in this book. They are explained in full in other books in these series. However, in a nutshell, the following definitions are used in this book:

- SLove (selfless love) is the purest kind of love we feel toward our children, Nature, and possibly for our artistic creations. We could also say that S stands for 'Serving.' With SLove, we Serve (give) love Selflessly.
- ELove (egotistic love) reflects the selfish need for love and attention and is mostly a reflection of insecurity. Alternately, E could stand for 'Expecting.' With ELove, we Expect (demand) love Egotistically.
- MLove (model love) is the tactful expressions of love to show compassion and cope with social etiquette. Alternately, M could stand for 'Moderating.' With MLove, we try to Moderate our relationships Modestly accordingly to a tactful Model.

Definitions of Four Personality Factors

The four personality factors shown in the Personality Chart reflect people's major urges to go around and do the things they do.

- **Instincts** drive many of our urges starting from the basic urge for sex all the way to the complex urge for spirituality. This factor reflects the *inner self* of a person.
- **Model** drives our urges to socialize and adapt. This factor reflects the *social orientation* of a person and his/her need for acceptance.
- **Ego** drives our urges to defend ourselves and to push our desires on others. This factor reflects the *object orientation* of a person, i.e., greed and a need to succeed in acquiring objects or dominating them.
- **Logic** drives our urges for decision making and planning. It reflects our ability to use our brain and the strength of our cognition. This factor reflects the *goal orientation* of a person.

Personality Chart and Ratings

The history of personality factors and ratings suggested in this book goes back a few decades to the time I was working on my Ph.D. in California and contemplating my dissertation. The hypotheses, design, and testing procedures were in place within a few months. A questionnaire was also developed for collecting information from the public, including the large population on the campus. Volunteers were asked to fill out a three-page questionnaire or sit for a fifteen-minute interview.

A preliminary study of the results, based on inputs from over hundred-fifty subjects, proved interesting for many purposes, but not quite for the main objective of measuring people's personality factors. It became apparent that subjects had become too over-conscious to reveal anything truthful about their personalities. This was equally true for both interviews and questionnaires. In fact, it appeared that the information the subjects provided was indeed the exact opposite of what it would have been if their brains could be read in a different manner or if they were connected to a lie detector. Everybody seemed eager to prove being the opposite of who s/he really was. Other than learning a great deal about humans' behaviour, especially during an interview or test, I built some form of intuition for reading between the lines that people delivered during the interviews or filling out a questionnaire.

In fact, it is rather easy for almost everybody to detect and measure other people's Model (a mix of flexibility and showiness) and Ego (a mix of doggedness and haughtiness). Once we have the ratings for Model and Ego for a person, we can calculate Instincts and Logic factors for him as well. Instincts and Logic are hard to detect and measure directly. However, my studies show that the rating for Instincts is normally a complement of Ego's rating (and adds up to 100). For example, if we rate a person's Ego at say 85, then his rating for Instincts would be 15. Similarly, the rating for Logic complements the rating for Model. Therefore, if the rating for his Model were, let us say, 65, then his rating for Logic would be 35. I usually use several criteria to arrive at Model and Ego ratings for a person, and then estimate the ratings for the Instincts and Logic for that person. Finally, I use some other criteria to make any last refinements that might seem necessary according to additional information available to me about that person.

The above hypotheses about the complementary nature of each pair of 'Ego and Instincts' and 'Model and Logic' have jumped up and become plausible from the results of the initial survey. It makes sense somewhat that the more we use our Ego, the more we dampen our instinctual urges and intuition. Equally reasonable is the assumption that our Logic is compromised faster (and we become more reckless), the more we get obsessed with adaptation and for being accepted in society at any cost—maybe even losing our integrity. The inherent interconnectivity of the four personality factors is intriguing, nevertheless, and I hope to find even more explanations for my hypotheses in the future.

Obviously, I could not justify my rather crude and subjective methodology for estimating the ratings for subjects' personality factors. It could not qualify for writing a scientific paper or dissertation, especially since many of my deductions contradicted the subjects' official answers. This is probably a valuable lesson any social scientist or human behaviour scholar learns: That with so little control over subjects' responses, we usually get unreliable data. We can make our questions as indirect and innovative as possible in hopes of distracting the subjects' mind from our intention. Still, people read between the lines and react even more creatively in their own ways. Overall, it seemed that neither my subjective assessments of subjects' personality, nor their direct responses could satisfy the validity and reliability requirements of the conclusions for my dissertation purposes.

Therefore, I choose a more mathematical dissertation topic to avoid the need for human input. At the same time, I was attracted to this personality model even more after facing people's natural resistance to be sincere even with themselves. Instead of discarding my pet project entirely, measuring humans' personalities remained a rather curious habit for me all along. Everybody is eager intuitively to judge every person s/he knows or meets even if it is only for ten minutes. I have been doing the same thing in the last thirty years, albeit a bit more scientifically, based on certain criteria that I developed early on and refined further through experience and analyses. I have also kept records of my personality ratings of others as much as possible, up to five subjects per week. I have rated friends, family members, colleagues, strangers, and the public, through simple interactions or during seminars and therapies. I have rated some people maybe 2-5 times over the years in their different life circumstances along various behavioural elements, e.g., degree of their decisiveness. These secondary information have been useful for various purposes, including the gender distinctions noted for the Gender Qualities and Symptoms.

This general background provides an insight about the source of the personality ratings used in this and my other books. The simplified Personality Chart presented on the next page shows the way four personality factors work together in order to present a person to others and in the society. A more elaborate personality chart and discussions are available in *The Nature of Love and Relationships* and a new book devoted to human personality will be released soon.

The upper part of the Chart (in the next page) shows the open side of our personality, the 'Conscious Individual.' Model and Ego factors of our personality help us portray our identity and individuality consciously.

The lower part of the Chart shows the 'Subconscious Self,' which is mostly the hidden aspect of our personality. Our instincts and logic are inner urges that drive us to live and do things intuitively, most often without being conscious of how they (instincts and common sense) are operating within us. Sometimes, we are aware and pay attention to our instincts and logic. This indicates that accessing our 'unconscious self' is not totally out of our reach. It simply requires more meditation and self-awareness.

Personality Chart

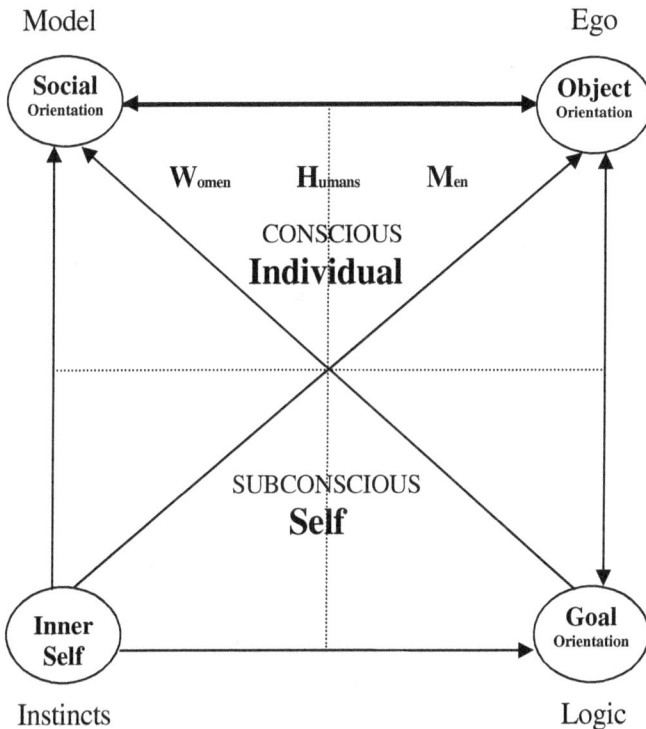

The point shown as 'Humans' at the top of the Chart offers an approximate rating for human personality. This rating means that an average human in modern society is only slightly driven by instincts (about 20% of all his/her instinctual capacities), s/he knows how to adapt to his/her environment by using his Model (on about 70% of occasions), s/he is highly self-centred and object-oriented (in about 80% of his/her dealings with people), and s/he benefits from logic and common sense to some extent (about 30% of his/her total potential). This rating is obviously too far off the ideal personality that can be imagined for a relatively good personality. Thus, using the above noted percentages, we can show the overall personality rating for humans as (20,70,80,30), which reflect their capacity for using their instincts, model, ego, and logic respectively.

Exploring the data a bit deeper, men and women with all types of personality ratings could be found anywhere on the Chart. However, it is probably safe to suggest the average ratings of (30,80,70,20) and (10,60,90,40) for women and men respectively. These two ratings are shown in the Chart at points noted as 'Women' and 'Men'.

An imaginary perfect human might be able to use 100% of every four factors and attain the highest levels of efficiency, effectiveness, and emotional capacity. In that bizarre society, human rating would be (100,100,100,100). Therefore, we can theoretically say that a perfect person could possibly earn 400 points, one point for every percent of personality factors. At the present time, it seems that people living in modern cultures get at best a total of 200 points, while the variations along their four personality factors remain drastically unbalanced and problematic. Humans can never reach 400, but even getting to 250 would be a great accomplishment if a better balance among the four factors are created as well.

Other Uses of the Personality Chart

1. The arrows in the Personality Chart indicate the following facts:

- Our instincts drive us to develop 'goal, social, and object' orientations. Thus, we develop Model and Ego and an ability to think and use logic.
- Our urges for goal orientation and object orientation constantly exchange information to support each other.
- Our urges for social orientation and object orientation constantly interact to empower each other.
- Social orientation and goal orientation also interact constantly, both directly and through object orientation. Nonetheless, all factors of personality interact amongst themselves constantly.
- The plausible inherent connectivity between Instincts and Ego and between Model and Logic (as shown by diagonal arrows in the chart) seem particularly intriguing and in need of more research.

2. The above personality chart can help for developing:
   a) Various tests for measuring each person's personality along the dimensions specified in the Chart.
   b) A standard for the 'balanced personality' only for the sake of making comparisons possible.
   c) Rules and principles about the ways personality ratings of individuals relate to their behaviour in relationships.
   d) Average rating for a common person.
   e) Rules and principles about the compatibility of couples' personalities for the sake of maximizing the effectiveness of their relationship.
   f) A rating for a normal person, who has the highest chance of relating effectively in his/her relationships. Most likely a relationship becomes successful if the couple has high personality (balanced) ratings, i.e., close to (50,50,50,50). However, it is interesting to develop theories about the possibility of other kinds of complemen-

tary or contradictory personalities corresponding in some types of relationships. Couples might be considered compatible for a particular relationship model according to their personality ratings.

A Recap of Personality Factors

Genders Qualities, and Symptoms

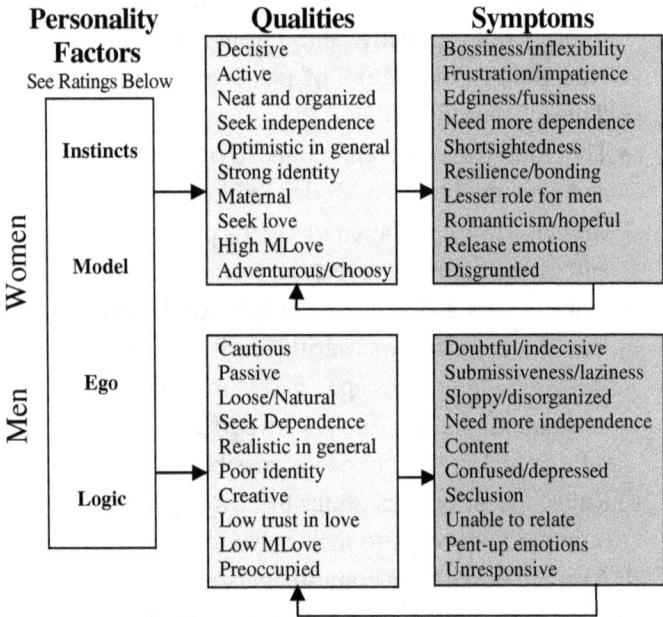

Personality Factors See Ratings Below	Qualities	Symptoms
Instincts **Model**	Decisive Active Neat and organized Seek independence Optimistic in general Strong identity Maternal Seek love High MLove Adventurous/Choosy	Bossiness/inflexibility Frustration/impatience Edginess/fussiness Need more dependence Shortsightedness Resilience/bonding Lesser role for men Romanticism/hopeful Release emotions Disgruntled
Ego **Logic**	Cautious Passive Loose/Natural Seek Dependence Realistic in general Poor identity Creative Low trust in love Low MLove Preoccupied	Doubtful/indecisive Submissiveness/laziness Sloppy/disorganized Need more independence Content Confused/depressed Seclusion Unable to relate Pent-up emotions Unresponsive

(Women / Men shown on left side)

Personality

Factors	Women	Men	Humans
Instincts	30%	10%	20%
Model	80%	60%	70%
Ego	70%	90%	80%
Logic	20%	40%	30%
Total Points	**200**	**200**	**200**

The diagram in the previous page is simply a collection of all the suggestions made about gender differences in Part I of this book.

Sample Personality Ratings

Over 2,000 personality ratings have been accumulated from various sources and settings by the author in the last few decades, especially the last ten years. A set of criteria has been applied to estimate each factor's rating, but the total score (for four ratings) is always forced to 200 points. The author is also planning to prepare a simple methodology for people to estimate their own or other people's personality ratings. Just to provide the readers with an insight, the ratings of eight familiar politicians are offered below. Their public speeches, demeanour, honesty, and decisions regarding citizens' welfare have provided the basis for these ratings. Make your own objective ratings about these authorities and compare. You can follow the methodology explained before, i.e., estimating Model and Ego first and then calculating the complementary ratings for Instincts and Logic—100 points for each pair.

	Instincts	Model	Ego	Logic
Stephen Harper:	(10,	85,	90,	15)
Thomas Mulcair:	(20,	75,	80,	25)
Justine Trudeau:	(30,	60,	70,	40)
Elizabeth May:	(40,	80,	60,	20)
Pierre Trudeau:	(20,	65,	80,	35)
John F. Kennedy:	(25,	60,	75,	40)
Rachel Notley:	(25,	75,	75,	25)
Barack Obama:	(35,	65,	65,	35)

The last two individuals on the above list were chosen from the personality ratings' archive because they offer good examples of better-balanced personality factors for the present era. They are also exceptional in the way their ratings are significantly different from their genders'. You can compare the above ratings with the average ratings that have been estimated by the author for humans and across genders so far in the bottom of page 192.